I have seen God's anointing operate through Judy Jacobs Tuttle to proclaim liberty to the captives. I know firsthand that this is a subject with which she is well acquainted. Her assignment, and one that she has wholeheartedly embraced, is to use the anointing to proclaim Jesus Christ as the resurrected King of glory, and see lives transformed as a result.

—Pastor Rod Parsley
World Harvest Church/Breakthrough

Judy Jacobs walks with God. Although she is most widely known as one of the world's foremost praise and worship leaders, she is also a gifted communicator of biblical truths. In this work she passes on principles that have worked for her, her children, her husband, Jamie, and the thousands they have discipled in the Scriptures. As you walk through the pages of this book, you will walk with one of this generation's true champions.

—Harry R. Jackson Jr.
Senior pastor, Hope Christian Church,
Beltsville, MD
President, High Impact Leadership Coalition
Presiding bishop, International Communion of
Evangelical Churches

Judy Jacobs is a sent one. She has been called for this hour to awaken the gifts and anointing that too often lie dormant in us. The Word of God through her life and pen wields a crushing blow to the spirit of fear and silences every excuse that keeps us from living in our full potential.

—Karen Wheaton
Founder and senior leader of The Ramp

Judy Jacobs can write about anointing because she is anointed. The anointing, as I understand it, is the bestowal of authorization by the Holy Spirit upon men and women to act in certain capacities.

When God anoints believers—as He has done with this fascinating young woman preacher/singer/author—they become

D1414076

equipped, enlightened, electrified, and empowered to accomplish what He puts in their hearts to do.

Knowledge and experience may help in the process, but it is only God's anointing that brings eternal results.

Thank you, Judy, for providing this practical and spiritual guide!

—T. L. LOWERY
EVANGELIST AND FOUNDER,
T. L. LOWERY GLOBAL FOUNDATION

Anointed and Judy Jacobs Tuttle have become synonymous with those who know anything about Judy's life and ministry. I have known Judy for most of her life. And after more than fifty years of personal ministry, I have a feeling I know something about anointing. Judy Jacobs Tuttle is anointed!

Anointing is something you simply can't impart to someone else. It is born out of prayer, commitment, dedication and obedience. Anointing is a personal matter. Judy has paid the price.

Trying to do God's work without anointing would be as futile as the son of the prophet in 2 Kings chapter 6 trying to chop wood with an ax handle after he had lost his cutting edge. *You Are Anointed for This!* gives us concrete guidance as to how to live and minister under the anointing.

—LAMAR VEST
PRESIDENT EMERITUS OF AMERICAN BIBLE SOCIETY
ASSOCIATE PASTOR, TIMES SQUARE CHURCH,
NEW YORK CITY
DIRECTOR OF CENTER FOR SPIRITUAL LEADERSHIP AND
RENEWAL, PENTECOSTAL THEOLOGICAL SEMINARY,
CLEVELAND, TN

YOU ARE ANOINTED FOR THIS!

JUDY JACOBS

CHARISMA
HOUSE

Most CHARISMA HOUSE BOOK GROUP products are available at special quantity discounts for bulk purchase for sales promotions, premiums, fund-raising, and educational needs. For details, write Charisma House Book Group, 600 Rinehart Road, Lake Mary, Florida 32746, or telephone (407) 333-0600.

YOU ARE ANOINTED FOR THIS! by Judy Jacobs
Published by Charisma House
Charisma Media/Charisma House Book Group
600 Rinehart Road
Lake Mary, Florida 32746
www.charismahouse.com

Unless otherwise noted, all Scripture quotations are from the New King James Version of the Bible. Copyright © 1979, 1980, 1982 by Thomas Nelson, Inc., publishers. Used by permission.

Scripture quotations marked AMP are from the Amplified Bible. Old Testament copyright © 1965, 1987 by the Zondervan Corporation. The Amplified New Testament copyright © 1954, 1958, 1987 by the Lockman Foundation. Used by permission.

Scripture quotations marked GNT are from the Good News Translation (formerly Today's English Version), copyright © 1992 by American Bible Society. Used by permission.

Scripture quotations marked HCSB are from the Holman Christian Standard Bible, copyright © 1999, 2000, 2002, 2003 by Holman Bible Publishers, Nashville, Tennessee. All rights reserved. Used by permission.

Scripture quotations marked ISV are from the Holy Bible: International Standard Version, copyright © 1996–2012 by The ISV Foundation of

Cover design by Justin Evans
Design Director: Bill Johnson

Visit the author's website at www.judyjacobs.com.

Library of Congress Cataloging-in-Publication Data:
Jacobs, Judy, 1957-
  You are anointed for this! / Judy Jacobs. -- First edition.
     pages cm
  Includes bibliographical references.
  ISBN 978-1-62136-282-1 (trade paper) -- ISBN 978-1-62136-283-8
(ebook)
  1. Anointing of the Holy Spirit. 2. Holy Spirit--Biblical teaching. I.
Title.

  BT123.J33 2013
  234'.13--dc23

                              2013016808

14 15 16 17 — 9 8 7 6 5 4 3
Printed in the United States of America

DEDICATION

I DEDICATE THIS BOOK first and foremost to my loving husband of twenty years, Pastor Jamie Tuttle. Babe, for more than twenty years you have been the very heartbeat of who we are simply because you believed in the anointing that was on the inside of me. It was you in the past twenty-five years who have constantly reminded me that, "You are anointed for this. Judy, you can do this." Many times I doubted, but you were always there with me, in the studio, behind the curtain, behind the sound system, and, yes, in the audience cheering me on. It would have been enough if only *I* had noticed it, but the *whole world* has seen who my *greatest cheerleader is—you, babe.* I will always cherish you and be grateful to God for bringing you into my life. I think you know who *your* greatest cheerleaders are. Yes, that would be me and your two girls. (Did I mention your mom also?)

I want to say thank you to the Jacobs and Tuttle families, who have always been a source of support and encouragement. To Danny and Debbie Murray, who always pushed the envelope to get me out of my comfort zone. To Steve and Pat Brock for making the phone call, and Pastor Benny Hinn and Pastor Rod Parsley for giving me a stage. Thank you, Paul and Jan Crouch, for introducing me to the world. Thank you, Steve and Joy Strang and Charisma Media, for giving me an amazing opportunity to share my revelations and stories. I also thank the many people who believed in the anointing that is on my life and continue to believe in the gifts in me. To my loving daughters, Kaylee and Erica, who allowed Mom to walk out this anointing in my life and for those who stayed and cared for them. I am eternally grateful!

To my Lord and Savior, Jesus Christ, and the blessed Holy Spirit who has given me the ministry and gifts to walk in this anointing and confidence and boldness. "For in Him we [I] live and move and have our [my] being" (Acts 17:28).

Finally I want to say to our loving church family, Dwelling Place Church International, in this final hour, you are anointed for this. To our mentors and mentees of the International Institute of Mentoring, you are anointed for this. To every believer who will read this revelation and have ever wondered and been unsure and uncertain if you are really and truly anointed and called, let me assure you, you are anointed for this!

CONTENTS

ACKNOWLEDGMENTS

N O ONE CAN do anything worthwhile or successful unless she has faithful friends who will come alongside of her to help her. Such is the case for all of the many people who contributed to this project.

To my covenant partners Perry and Pam Stone, who have been such a blessing in our lives, I want to say thank you from my heart. Your uncanny support has been truly amazing and radical in a world that is turned so inward. Jamie and I cherish this covenant and always will, until Jesus comes back.

To Pastor Rod and Joni Parsley, who gave us our very first stage on international television. Talking about being "anointed for this," nine months pregnant at Dominion Camp Meeting, they had to surely believe in the anointing on my life. You are still my favorite!

To Steve and Joy Strang, the Charisma House family, my "anointed" editor, Jevon Bolden, and the Charisma House editors, I say thank you and a very well-done job on the final manuscript.

To all the friends, artists, pastors, and leaders who shared with us your interpretation and revelation of the anointing, my heartfelt thanks for your time and effort put forth and for telling us your life witness of the precious Holy Spirit in your own words.

To a covenant friend who helped me burn the midnight oil and the midday oil, Mrs. Kathie Kennemer, and my lifelong friends, my husband, the Milligans, and the Potters, with whom in one weekend I received enough revelation to write eighteen books. Whew! Those preachers! Love you! To Amanda Fisher, who helped get the final edit out: I never would have made it without your help.

FOREWORD

THE ANOINTING! JUST the word alone paints numerous images in the minds of believers. Is the anointing an emotion released in the excitement of a powerful worship experience? Is it the energy felt when a minister preaches with a divine unction? Is the anointing a spiritual charge in the atmosphere that can be felt by the attendees when prayer is being offered?

Our perception of what is or is not the anointing often stems from our upbringing in a local church, teaching from the pulpit, or what we view through denominational glasses. However, in both Testaments the anointing was the very energy and life of God manifested through the voices of the prophets, priests, and righteous kings. David was anointed on three occasions: by Samuel as a teen, by the men of Judah, and as king over Israel at age thirty. He spoke of being "anointed with fresh oil" (Ps. 92:10). Thus, with each new level a fresh anointing is required.

It takes an anointed servant of the Lord to write about the anointing. A theologian and scholar can break down Greek and Hebrew words, but only an anointed individual can express what the anointing is, how it operates, and why it is required to "break the yokes" in our lives (Isa. 10:27). Such a person is Judy Jacobs, known around the world as an anointed handmaiden of the Lord.

I have known Judy from the early days when she sang with a traveling ministry from Lee College (now Lee University) and have followed her ministry over the years and watched the favor of God as He released His blessing and increased His anointing upon her and her husband Jamie's lives. On the subject of the anointing she clearly knows of which she speaks, and through this book you too will discover the secrets of being anointed for your end-time assignments! Through the anointing your "this" will become "that," and "that" is what will make a difference in your "this"! As Peter declared, "This is that" (Acts 2:16, KJV).

—Perry Stone
International evangelist and host of *Manna-fest*

PREFACE

IT WAS DURING the spring quarter of my senior year at Emmanuel College. I was completing my biblical studies degree and preparing to graduate. As a student, I was on a work study program, and my job was being the chapel sound man, along with several other media responsibilities.

I remember as if it were yesterday: Thursday morning, 10:00 a.m., and students were gathered for what was to be an "exciting" college chapel service. The guest that day was a recruiting group from Lee College (now Lee University) of Cleveland, Tennessee, and they were there to sing and minister as well as present Lee to all the junior college graduates. Obviously, being a senior in the Bible school, I didn't think this chapel would apply to me. I was only there to fulfill my work responsibility—or so I thought.

That morning would be the day that changed my life forever. You see, throughout my college days I always kept a prayer list in my Bible. Every day I would go down my list, presenting my needs and desires to God. I included the basics of most young men in a Christian college: "Lord, help me pass my Greek test," and, "Lord, please, I need money." However, there was one request that was much more descriptive than others: "Lord, this is what I desire in a wife…"

The first part wasn't very spiritual; it was a typical prayer: "Lord, I would really like her to have dark skin, brown eyes, and black or brown hair." Then I got more spiritual and prayed, "May she be able to sing and pray like my mom. Lord, I want her to love You more than me and desire Your presence and power more than anything. Give me a wife who has a heart for the nations." I really can't remember if I had prayed yet on that Thursday, but unbeknownst to me, the answer to my prayers walked out on the stage for chapel.

Six years later, after pursuing a music passion, a masters of divinity degree in marriage and family, and serving a year in Florida as a youth pastor, I married Judy Jacobs, the girl of my dreams and prayers. We embarked upon a journey of ministry that we simply never expected. And now, twenty years later, we have learned that absolutely nothing is more important than the anointing of Almighty God upon our lives and family. As a matter of fact, we learned very early that if there is no anointing, it's all just a bunch of noise and powerless actions. For it is the power, the fuel, the strength, the supply, the provision, and even the fire and boldness that rises up in you at different moments in life. We have traveled to more than thirty countries; seen thousands of people receive Christ; and sat before prime ministers, presidents, and dignitaries—all because of His anointing upon our lives.

As Judy's husband, friend, partner in ministry, manager, sound man, sometimes drummer, and even bus driver (that's right), I have seen her stand before just a few people or three quarters of a million people and declare, "THERE'S NO GOD LIKE JEHOVAH," knowing that her preparation for either venue was the same: "Father, I simply can't do this in myself, but through You and Your anointing upon my life, I can do anything. Your anointing upon my life is all that matters, and You have equipped me for what I am about to do." You see, one thing I've learned from her, while ministering alongside of her, is that she is always ministering before an audience of ONE: "Will He be pleased? Will He be glorified with my life?"

Judy has always known the price of the anointing upon her life; it's a sacrifice. In order to really be who God has called you to be, it takes being set apart: where you deny self, surrounding influences, persuasions, and personalities, and then abandon yourself to Him.

The book you hold in your hands is not just a manual for simple learning, but rather it's a life-changing work, full of scriptural revelation, written by one who has lived the ups and downs of the experiences in the anointing. You and I both know that not every day is the best day, but one thing is for sure: when God calls you out with a purpose and a plan, you can rest assured that *you are anointed for this!*

—Jamie Tuttle

Introduction

GOD'S ANOINTING IS *for* YOU

And it shall come to pass in the last days, says God, that I will pour
out of My Spirit on all flesh; your sons and your daughters shall
prophesy, your young men shall see visions, your old men shall
dream dreams. And on My menservants and on My maidservants
I will pour out My Spirit in those days; and they shall prophesy.

—ACTS 2:17–18

I F THERE IS one thing I have learned during my life span on
this earth so far, it is that God is constantly trying to get us
through a "this" so He can get us to a "that." I'm reminded
of the Upper Room experience quoted above, where Peter told the
onlookers, "But *this* is *that* which was spoken by the prophet Joel"
(Acts 2:16, KJV, emphasis added).

This is what I know: there is a place in the spirit realm where
every believer longs to go, and when we get to *that* place, we don't
want to leave. We want to dwell there. "Where is *that* place?" you
might ask. That place is *in the anointing.*

Men and women of God have operated in the anointing
throughout eons of time. While being eaten by lions, they sang;
while being blindfolded and waiting for bullets to fire through
their entire bodies, they prayed in peace; and as Stephen was being
stoned, he looked up to heaven and asked God, "Lord, lay not this

sin to their charge" (Acts 7:60, kjv). These saints of God paid the ultimate price for their commitment to the cause of the anointing. We as the church long to be infiltrated with it more and more in our lives.

So what is the anointing? What does it look like? Why are some people seemingly anointed and others aren't? How can you get the anointing? What will it do for your life? Is it just for people who are in full-time ministry—apostles, prophets, evangelists, pastors, and teachers—those who are seemingly very, very spiritual?

These are questions God's people have frequently asked, passionately motivated to find the right answers for themselves. They have grappled with these questions and longed to experience the anointing, yet many of them still feel left out in the dark on this subject. The Questions rumble in their minds over and over again: *How can I be anointed? I know others are, but what about me?*

In this book all of these questions will be answered and lots more. I believe as you read that the Holy Spirit is going to make things crystal clear to you about the anointing upon your life. Yes, you read it right. *The anointing upon your life.* My friend, God has anointed you! You just need to believe and receive your impartation through this *now* word that God has given to me for you.

You see, the days we are living in are unprecedented in every respect, yet not surprising. These are the days and times that the prophets, the inspired writers of the Holy Scriptures, and even Jesus Himself warned would come. Things such as:

- Wars and rumors of wars

- The rise of lawlessness

- Apostasy

- Economic and environmental disasters

- Dramatic political, social, cultural, medical, and moral changes

These are, as 2 Timothy 3:1 confirms, "perilous [dangerous] times." Yet even in these times God is still active in His church. He is still moving mightily on people whose hearts are turned toward Him. As we look toward the ultimate escape from all of this mess, we—the people of God and the bride of Christ—are keeping our focus on Jesus, the author and finisher of our faith. We are in a battle for everything that we know is right, and as a community of believers, as a nation, as families, and ultimately as people who know their God, we are confident that our victory is sure. Yet I believe before the return of the Lord the things that can be shaken are being removed "that the things which cannot be shaken may remain" (Heb. 12:27).

I believe this is the time that God is raising up many anointed men and women of God to change societies and cultures as we know them. "How do we change them?", you might ask. We change them through the name of Jesus and through the living Word of God. We appropriate the blood of Christ and use the power of agreement, believing that God hears and answers every prayer that we pray to Him in faith.

Most of all we use *the anointing* that God has given to every believer through the power of His Holy Spirit to stand up in the midst of a perverse and wicked generation and declare His Word.

In the book *Personal Faith, Public Policy* he cowrote with Tony Perkins, Bishop Harry R. Jackson says that we as the church must yield "to the ultimate truth test—not what do Republicans or conservatives say or Democrats or liberals think, but rather what does God's Word say."[1]

Everyone has the capacity to be anointed. God is no respecter of persons. The anointing is for every believer: every man, woman, boy, and girl. It is for the young. It is for the old. It is for the rich, and it is for the poor. It is for the one who is near and the one who is far off. The anointing is for you, your children, your children's children, and "as many as the Lord our God will call" (Acts 2:39).

Now, you must first realize one thing. The enemy will come and tell you, "You are not good enough to have the anointing on your life." He'll tell you that because you are divorced, or you didn't come from a family in the ministry, or you are not a perfect person that you can't experience the anointing. He'll constantly say to you, "Don't you remember when…?" Friend, don't ever forget this one fact: the devil is a liar!

The only thing you have to remember is the anointing that comes upon you is not *your anointing*. It is *God's anointing*, the anointing of the Holy Spirit. God is the one who gives His anointing to us. It is a free gift that comes directly from Him, and once given, it is to be shared with others. The anointing doesn't belong to your mama, your dad, your grandma, or your auntie. The anointing belongs to God.

His anointing destroys the yoke of cancer. It annihilates the HIV/AIDS virus. God's anointing releases healings, deliverances, miracles, signs, and wonders. But this same anointing also helps you live out your everyday life as one of the called-out, chosen, and appointed people of God.

You Are Anointed to Do "Greater Works"

You also need to understand that God wants His people to walk in the supernatural revelation of what He sent Jesus to the earth to do: "For this purpose the Son of God was manifested, that He might destroy the works of the devil" (1 John 3:8). Jesus's purpose on earth was to ultimately destroy the enemy's works in people's lives and to set every captive free. That's why He, the sinless Lamb of God, was slain from the foundation of the world (Rev. 13:8). When He left the earth, He handed it down to us. Sometimes people like to take credit for the anointing, but always remember Romans 11:36, which states: "For of Him and through Him and to Him are all things, to whom [God the Father, God the Son, and God the Holy Ghost] be glory forever. Amen."

When Jesus told the disciples to go to the Upper Room and wait for the "Promise of the Father" (Acts 1:4), He knew they were going to do the works that He had done, and even greater works. How do I know this? He had already told them, "He who believes in Me, the works that I do he will do also; and greater works than these he will do, because I go to My Father" (John 14:12). I believe this book will give you boldness, power, authority, divine inspiration, and revelation to do "greater works" as you receive and flow in the Lord's anointing.

There is another understanding you must have about the anointing, and it comes from Isaiah 61. Jesus declared this to the religious leaders of His day as He stood in the synagogue to read from the scroll of the prophet Isaiah. He boldly said:

> The Spirit of the LORD is upon Me, because He has anointed Me to preach the gospel to the poor; He has sent Me to heal the brokenhearted, to proclaim liberty to the captives and recovery of sight to the blind, to set at liberty those who are oppressed; to proclaim the acceptable year of the LORD.
> —LUKE 4:18–19

When Jesus declared those words about His own works in the earth, by extension He was also talking about the "greater works" that would be done by the disciples, and ultimately you and me. *This book will help you to understand that the Lord's anointing is for you, right now, and for such a time as this.*

The anointing is not for those who you might think are deemed worthy of it. Rather, this revelation and word will help you to see that the anointing comes from God through the power of the Holy

Spirit, and it is for anyone who will seek after it, cradle it with all humility, and guard it. This anointing, as spoken of in Ephesians 4, is for "the equipping of the saints for the work of ministry, for the edifying of the body of Christ, till we all come into the unity of the faith and of the knowledge of the Son of God, to a perfect man, to the measure of the stature of the fullness of Christ" (vv. 12–13).

That means YOU! With this revelation in your heart and mind you will begin to decree and declare, "The Spirit of the Lord is upon ME, because the Lord has anointed ME!"

God has gifted the body of Christ with many supernatural gifts, and He wants you to use every gift He has given you to advance His kingdom with others and see lives changed through the power of the gospel. So whatever gifts you may have, in whatever capacity, and wherever you feel God has called you, I urge you to use those gifts, *because YOU are anointed for this!*

You Are Anointed for Victory

There is something else that the anointing is for: to help you understand that whatever you may be facing—be it a trial, hardship, or difficulty; a calling; or anything you feel you aren't able to handle or come out of—God wants you to know *you are anointed for this!*

You might be going through a particularly hard season right now in your finances. You need to know that *you are anointed for this!* By God's power and grace, His Word declares, "And my God shall supply all your need according to His riches in glory by Christ Jesus" (Phil. 4:19). King David said, "I have been young, and now am old; yet have I not seen the righteous forsaken, nor His seed begging bread" (Ps. 37:25, KJV). You're coming out of this! There is an anointing upon you to believe God for the unbelievable!

You might have received a bad report from your doctor. You need to understand, *you are anointed for this!* Whose report will you believe? *Say it:* "I will believe the report of the Lord." Jesus said,

"*All things are possible* to him who believes" (Mark 9:23, emphasis added). He said on another occasion, "With men this is impossible, but with God *all things are possible*" (Matt. 19:26, emphasis added). You are anointed to get the victory over this illness and come out as the healed of the Lord. God is going to anoint you to increase your level of faith to believe for a miracle.

You might be in the fight of your life for your marriage, your children, or your home—so believe this one thing: *You are anointed for this!* God is going to give you the extra grace and glory you need to believe Him for a miracle.

For everything that you are facing right now, there is an anointing…to face it, overcome it, restore it, transform it, and see dynamic change. Why? The Spirit of the Lord God is upon you! He has anointed you, so your "this" becomes "that" which was spoken of by the prophet Joel. Because God is pouring out His Spirit upon your life, *you are anointed for this!* You can come out of every challenge in victory.

With this in mind, as you finish each chapter, make sure to do the closing exercise. God wants you to experience His anointing as you never have before. I urge you: take time to make this journey into the anointing personal. God wants to do "greater works," both *in* and *through* you.

Get ready to come face-to-face with an anointing that you never knew was possible, simply because you'll recognize and declare, "Hey, you know what? The Spirit of the Lord God IS upon ME, and He has anointed ME for this! The same power that raised Jesus from the dead is in ME; I am anointed to do 'greater works' in His name!" I prophesy to you that after reading this book, you are going to find yourself completely overwhelmed with confidence, boldness, and authority that you never dreamed possible. Why? *YOU ARE ANOINTED FOR THIS!*

one

IN *the* BEGINNING

Then God said, "Let there be…"

—GENESIS 1:3

THE WORD *ANOINTING* is associated with many things in the Word of God. So we're going to take some time to break it down. No matter how far along you are in the river of the anointing, you will be able to understand what it is in its fullest sense. You see, oftentimes we judge people because they're either not as "deep" as we may be or aren't farther along in their relationship with God. I have found out that, as believers, we must be very mindful of one another. Someone once said, "Be careful how you judge people in their seeming simplicity; remember, God became a baby."

One thing God has constantly helped me to understand in my life is the power of one little word—*yes*. It is a small word, but it carries a great punch. I think of Mary, the mother of Jesus, and how huge that word must have been for her. Sure, God had a plan B for back up, but Mary chose to say, "Let it be to me according to your will" (Luke 1:38).

Are you hungry to experience more of the anointing? I have good news. God has already spoken the "Let there be…" to you for your life. If you haven't responded to the Lord, He's waiting for you to say, just as Mary did, "Yes, let it be to *me* according to Your Word." You will discover as the revelation of this book unfolds in your life that you'll constantly be in a place where He is challenging you to say these very words.

If you plan to walk in your destiny in God and grow in the anointing, like Jesus, you will *learn obedience* from the Father. (See Hebrews 5:8.) God is looking for you to say yes to Him without hesitation. One thing I know about God is that He hears and answers sincere prayers. If you are brutally honest and tell God how much you want the anointing, you will see things begin to open up within you and in your circumstances that will absolutely astound you.

I get really amused at people who come to me sometimes with all sincerity and say, "Sister Judy, I really want God to use me. I really want His anointing operating in my life, but I just want the Holy Spirit to do it very gently and in my way…I don't want to fall out in the Spirit and be embarrassed—but I am really hungry for the anointing of God in my life."

I always say to them, "I am just going to pray and let God do what He wants…do you agree with that?" And they usually answer, "Oh, yes! That is exactly what I want—what God wants." Then oftentimes when I pray, I don't even lay a hand on them. Most fall out under the power of the anointing, face first. When they get up, their hair is messed up, their makeup is running, and they can't walk or talk. But yet they are the most joyful people in the room.

Praise God! That's what a living encounter with the Holy Spirit's anointing will do! When God's *super* touches your *natural*—when the Father's glory (His "*kābôd*," His heaviness[1]) meets your human flesh—there's no way you can stand under that supernatural anointing.

Sometimes when we experience those glory times with God, we

get excited and begin to make all kinds of promises to Him; we start saying "Let there be…" to Him. There's nothing wrong with that, but always remember: while there are times we humans forget, *God never forgets*. What you promised Him two, three, or more years down the road in your past, He remembers. And at some point HE WILL remind you of those things.

THE GENESIS OF THE ANOINTING

There's only one place to start when it comes to talking about the anointing, and that is from the beginning. Jewish tradition holds that Moses is the author of the first five books of the Bible, which begins with the Book of Genesis. Moses, under the direct anointing of God, was divinely inspired to bring into account every biblical fact and principle that has been under scrutiny by secular humanism, atheism, Darwinism, and any other "ism" since the beginning of the human race.

But the truth still remains…in the beginning was God: God the Father, God the Son, and God the Holy Ghost. And by the way, they are still very much alive today! Muhammad (the founder of Islam) is dead. Allah (the god of Islam) is dead. Krishna (the god of Hinduism) is dead—but Jesus was, is, and will always be alive. He is alive forevermore.

I believe that when God said "Let there be…," the entire host of heaven, including the angels, was involved in Creation. Genesis opens with the arrangement of the solar system, the separation of the waters, and the forming of land for habitation for what was coming…man! Then after completing His prized creations, God blessed Adam and Eve and told them:

> Be fruitful and multiply; fill the earth and subdue it; have dominion over the fish of the sea, over the birds of the air, and over every living thing that moves on the earth.
>
> —GENESIS 1:28

So from the beginning God appointed us sons and daughters of the first Adam, and then by faith we became sons and daughters of God, brothers and sisters of the second Adam, Jesus Christ, as heirs to this earth domain. (See 1 Corinthians 15:22, 45–50.) *We were made to dominate, reproduce, multiply, and replenish the earth with godly seed.* That power and anointing was rightfully given to us by God in the beginning, as descendants of His first creations, and today we have that authority to do the same in every sphere of our lives.

How do I know this? The Bible declares in Acts 10:38, "God anointed Jesus of Nazareth with the Holy Spirit and with power, who went about doing good and healing all who were oppressed by the devil, for God was with Him." Now if God anointed Jesus and we belong to Him, then we can know for sure He has anointed us. The Scriptures themselves (our final authority) prove and qualify this by saying:

> If the Spirit of God, who raised Jesus from death, lives in you, then he who raised Christ from death will also give life to your mortal bodies by the presence of his Spirit in you.
>
> —Romans 8:11, GNT

In fact, when we see the word *Christ* in the Scriptures, it identifies Jesus as "the Anointed One." We'll get to this in chapter 2.

THE GENESIS PRINCIPLE

Just as God anointed us from the beginning, He set a principle in place that governs how His anointing is released. A contemporary translation of the Scriptures describes what happened at the beginning of Creation this way:

First this: God created the Heavens and Earth—all you see, all you don't see. Earth was a soup of nothingness, a bottomless emptiness, an inky blackness. God's Spirit brooded like a bird above the watery abyss. God spoke, "Light!" And light appeared. God saw that the light was good and separated light from dark. God named the light Day, he named the dark Night. It was evening, it was morning—Day One.

—GENESIS 1:1–5, THE MESSAGE

I love how Eugene Peterson, the author of *The Message*, set up the "nothingness" of earth before God released His power to create the universe. Now let's see the beginning from reading Genesis 1:2 in the Amplified Bible:

The earth was without form and an empty waste, and darkness was upon the face of the very great deep. The Spirit of God was moving (hovering, brooding) over the face of the waters.

No matter how you shake it, in the midst of empty waste, nothingness, bottomless emptiness, and the inky blackness of a very great deep…something amazing happened: *God began to speak*. The words were simple, yet extremely powerful and of great magnitude:

Let there be…

—GENESIS 1:3, EMPHASIS ADDED

I put these words at the beginning of this chapter and repeated them here because this is the Genesis principle. *This* is *that*, which God declared through the prophet Joel would happen in the last days—because it happened in the beginning. God poured out His Spirit then, and He's pouring out His Spirit as you read at this very moment. *I declare to you: this book stands to inform you that before the foundations of the earth, God has already spoken His Word into your life. He has already declared, "Let there be…"*

Just as you have been anointed from the beginning as a descendant of the first and second Adam, you have also inherited the Genesis principle. That's why I believe with every fiber of my being that if you're not saying it, you won't see it. In other words, if you don't open your mouth and begin to speak "Let there be…" in the inky black situations of life, you won't see God pour out His Spirit, transforming darkness into light and nothingness into life.

You are anointed for this! Friend, you have faith in Jesus, so you can believe everything the Father, Son, and Holy Spirit have already done for you. Hebrews 11:1 says, "Now faith is the substance of things hoped for, the evidence of things not seen." Father God spoke Creation in motion by the power of His anointing, and the entire host of heaven immediately said yes and got busy! The spirit of faith is: "I believe; therefore I speak." (See 2 Corinthians 4:13.) *We speak because we have faith in God.*

Because of the Genesis principle, the words you speak are powerful. And they can have either a positive or negative effect. Jesus said:

> A good man out of the good treasure of his heart brings forth good things, and an evil man out of the evil treasure brings forth evil things. But I say to you that for every idle word men may speak, they will give account of it in the day of judgment. For by your words you will be justified, and by your words you will be condemned.
>
> —Matthew 12:35–37

Will You Declare, "Let It Be…"?

When God declares, "Let there be…" our response should always be, as I said at the beginning of this chapter, "Let it be unto me according to Your Word." If you want to know how God feels about your situation or dilemma, it is as simple as going to the Word.

> "The word is near you, in your mouth and in your heart" (that is, the word of faith which we preach).
> —ROMANS 10:8

> The lips of the [uncompromisingly] righteous know [and therefore utter] what is acceptable, but the mouth of the wicked knows [and therefore speaks only] what is obstinately willful and contrary.
> —PROVERBS 10:32, AMP

> You are snared by the words of your mouth; you are taken by the words of your mouth.
> —PROVERBS 6:2

> Take control of what I say, O LORD, and guard my lips.
> —PSALM 141:3, NLT

Jesus is the Word made flesh. (See John 1:1–9, 14.) The Word was, is, and forevermore will be our final authority. I don't care what a situation looks like, how it feels, or how long it may seem it could last; we must line up our words with the infallible true and living Word of God.

So I say again: We must *learn obedience* as Jesus did when He came to earth...and this starts with saying what the Word says about us. Then the anointing goes to work, both in us and through us, bringing everything into alignment with the Word of God. That's why the Bible says, "Let the weak say, 'I am strong'" (Joel 3:10). We can extend this principle into other areas of life, such as finances, declaring that we are rich because of what God has provided for us. (See Philippians 4:19.)

That's why Psalm 107:2 tells us, "Let the redeemed of the LORD say so" (emphasis added)! Need I say more? Jesus said, "Whoever *says* to this mountain, 'Be removed and be cast into the sea,' and does not doubt in his heart, but believes that those things he *says* will come to pass, he will have whatever he *says*" (Mark 11:23, emphasis added). *The Word can't get any more emphatic than that.*

Declaring "Let it be unto me…" to God's Word is saying a resounding *yes* to the Lord. I was reminded of two prominent women in the Bible as I was writing this chapter. One was willing to say yes, and the other doubted and even lied after God had promised her a special gift.

Let's look at the first woman, Mary. Many scholars believe that she was a very beautiful young lady of in her early teens when the angel came and "said to her, 'Rejoice, highly favored one, the Lord is with you; blessed are you among women!' But when she saw him, she was troubled at his saying, and considered what manner of greeting this was" (Luke 1:28–29).

At this point the world was in a terrible predicament and needed a Savior. We all know this story well, and we know Mary's response from earlier in this chapter. But let's walk through the process a little. As Mary listened to the angel, thinking deeply about the repercussions this would bring, she "counted the cost" and determined there was only one thing for her to say: "Behold the maidservant of the Lord! Let it be to me according to your word" (v. 38).

Let me put her response another way: "Lord, I don't know what this is going to be like, what everyone will think, especially Joseph, or how this is going to turn out—all I know is, I believe what I've been told. I agree with Your word." And the anointing of God went to work.

Many believers know what God has spoken—prophesied, decreed, and declared—over their lives. Yet many still wonder about, doubt, and analyze God's revealed word to them, trying to cross every *t* and dot every *i*…but let that not be said of you and me! God is saying, "Come on in; the water feels good. Just jump.

I'm going to catch you. Don't worry about what people think. Just get in the river of My anointing and see how glorious it will be to walk on water."

What would have happened if Mary had not said yes? I'll tell you what would have happened: God would have moved on to someone else, because the work of the Lord *must go on*, either with or without us. Young Mary was willing to say yes to God, in spite of the unknown, and follow His leading. Thousands of years later she is honored because of it.

There was another woman who was faced with a challenge and predicament that were a test of her faith. That woman was *Sarah*, a name God had given her because she would become "a mother of nations" (Gen. 17:15–16). But she doubted the promise that God had given her husband, Abraham. God had promised him that from his seed would come nations as his inheritance. (See Genesis 17:4–5, 18–19). He had promised him even before this, "This one [Eliezer] shall not be your heir, but one who will come from your own body shall be your heir....Look now toward heaven, and count the stars if you are able to number them....So shall your descendants be" (Gen. 15:4–5).

The angel of the Lord later appeared to Abraham and declared to him, "I will surely return to you about this time next year, and Sarah your wife will have a son" (Gen. 18:10, NIV).

When the angel announced this to Abraham, Sarah was hiding behind them at the entrance of the tent. She overheard that word, and the Bible says:

> So she laughed silently to herself and said, "How could a worn-out woman like me enjoy such pleasure, especially when my master—my husband—is also so old?" Then the LORD said to Abraham, "Why did Sarah laugh? Why did she say, 'Can an old woman like me have a baby?' Is

anything too hard for the LORD? I will return about this time next year, and Sarah will have a son."

—GENESIS 18:12–14, NLT

I thought it was interesting that God played off of the words Sarah used to describe herself, which lets us know that *He is a God of details.* That is why Jesus said we would give account for every idle word we speak on Judgment Day. Verse 15 says, "Sarah was afraid, so she denied it, saying, 'I didn't laugh.' But the LORD said, 'No, you did laugh'" (NLT). Sarah did become a mother of nations *because Abraham believed God,* yet thousands of years later we are able to see through her testimony just how serious God is about His Word.

Now let me ask you a serious question. Have you been laughing at what God has spoken, prophesied, promised, and/or declared over your life through His Word? Has a prophet, pastor, evangelist you know, or even a total stranger spoken the word of the Lord to you that resonated within your very being? You can make one of two choices: (1) You can laugh and say, "That's crazy. That will never happen to me," or (2) You can say, as Mary did, "Be it unto me according to Your Word."

At some point you will have to start saying, "Let it be to me according to Your Word, Lord. Whatever You have for me, I am ready." I declare to you today, LET IT BE!

- Going to the nations…*Let it be!*

- Starting a homeless ministry…*Let it be!*

- Starting your own business to finance the kingdom…*Let it be!*

- Witnessing to your neighbors…*Let it be!*

- Starting a Bible study at work…*Let it be!*

- Financing this "last day" outpouring…*Let it be!*

Something happened to me several years ago that I will never forget. My husband and I had gone to hear this fired-up evangelist and had brought along a friend. We were excited. We were really hungry for more of God and knew the minister operated in the prophetic. We had been praying and seeking the Lord and felt strongly that God had some amazing things for us to do and incredible doors He was going to open.

The service was so awesome, just as we had expected it to be. It was getting to the end, and we still had not received a word, but we weren't sweating it; we had a sure word from God and didn't really need a word from a man. But to be very honest, I was telling the Lord, "It sure would be nice, though, if we could get a confirmation."

As I was thinking that, all of a sudden, he called out the person who had come with us and began to prophesy all of these amazing things over him. I'm telling you, I was so excited to hear everything that was being said for this other person. Then, just as suddenly, the attention shifted to Jamie and me. He began to say, "I see long-stretched limos. I see large arenas. I see TV cameras everywhere. I see you before mighty men: presidents, prime ministers, people of great importance." As he began to say all of these things, it was such a confirmation in our spirits of what God had told us in the "secret place" of prayer. So we began to rejoice over the word of the Lord and began to call it in even more forcefully.

As soon as we got in our vehicle to leave the meeting, this other person began to make light of, even fun of, the word of the Lord, talking about how foolish and silly it was to hear all of that coming out of this man's mouth. We warned him to be careful, because you have to honor the word of the Lord when it is spoken in all sincerity, especially by a man or woman of God. I can tell you from that night on God began to do mighty works in our lives and ministry.

Jamie and I believed and claimed the promises of the word of the Lord spoken over us and began to call those things that be not as though they were. I can honestly tell you everything that this gentleman prophesied for us has come to pass and more.You might ask, "What about the other person?" I am sorry to say that because of his unbelief, he missed out on what God had for him. Today he lives a broken and unfulfilled life in ministry, especially concerning what was prophesied over him. What happened? We believed and received everything God said would happen and he didn't. One of us laughed at the word of the Lord and said, "That's so absurd and stupid. That will never happen." And it didn't. The others said, "Let it be unto us according to Your will, O God!" And everything came to pass!

As we continue learning about the anointing, you have to be willing to say yes to God and really mean it. Here's the thing: when you say yes, God knows if you are totally sincere because He knows your heart; so you might as well go ahead and be honest with Him the first time. He's waiting for you to believe and respond. Be like Mary and say yes, without doubt or hesitation. *You are anointed for this!*

∞ LET IT BE *to* ME . . .

What is the "Let there be…" God has spoken over your life? How did you respond to Him? Did you believe as Mary did and say yes, or did you think of everything that could possibly go wrong and reject His promise? Did you say yes as Abraham did, or did you hide and laugh like Sarah, thinking of your past mistakes and the time you've lost because of them? Maybe you said yes, but for some reason you stopped believing and obediently following God after you received His promise for your life.

Take a little time and go to the Lord in prayer. First John

1:9 says, "If we confess our sins, He is faithful and just to forgive us our sins and to cleanse us from all unrighteousness." Go, confess, be cleansed, and be set free! I agree with you in the name of Jesus that you will say to the Lord with your whole heart, "Let it be to me according to Your Word," and jump into the river of the anointing…*because you are anointed for this!*

two

WHAT IS *the* ANOINTING?

So He came to Nazareth, where He had been brought up. And
as His custom was, He went into the synagogue on the Sabbath
day, and stood up to read. And He was handed the book of
the prophet Isaiah. And when He had opened the book, He
found the place where it was written: "The Spirit of the Lord
is upon Me, because He has anointed Me to preach the gospel
to the poor; He has sent Me to heal the brokenhearted, to pro-
claim liberty to the captives and recovery of sight to the blind, to
set at liberty those who are oppressed; to proclaim the accept-
able year of the Lord." Then He closed the book, and gave it
back to the attendant and sat down. And the eyes of all who
were in the synagogue were fixed on Him. And He began to say
to them, "Today this Scripture is fulfilled in your hearing."

—LUKE 4:16–21

WHAT IS THE anointing? It is joy, passion, power, glory, confidence, boldness, and authority. It makes you cry. It makes you laugh. It gives you righteous indignation. It is the power to preach, sing, witness, testify, and do spiritual warfare. It is peace. It comes suddenly, and it takes time. It is meek, and it is strong. The anointing will come to get you through the death of a loved one, the rebellion of a child, the midnight of a divorce, the challenge of a special-needs child, or the pain of a suffering parent or loved one.

Some of these descriptions sound almost like an oxymoron; for example, fried ice or, more aptly in Scripture, a servant-king or the Son of God who is both man and God. The anointing is embodied and fulfilled in Jesus Christ, who opened the Scriptures and read Isaiah's prophecy, publicly declaring to the Father and all who were in the synagogue, "Let it be to Me according to Your Word."

His words caused a stir that day, so much so that the people were filled with wrath and threw Him out of the city, wanting to stone Him. But the story tells us that Jesus "went His way" to Capernaum, a city in Galilee, and started operating in the fullness of the anointing. (See Luke 4:28–37.) Talk about a contradiction! This same Christ, the Anointed One, also said, "Whoever seeks to save his life will lose it, and whoever loses his life will preserve it" (Luke 17:33). When the anointing comes, it creates a divine paradox—just as it did at the beginning of Creation. Light exposes darkness. Truth confronts lies. Life confronts death. Everything that can be shaken is removed so the things that can't be shaken will remain.

So how can we explain the anointing? Allow me to try.

While attending college, I was embarrassed one day when someone asked me, "Judy Jacobs, can you describe the anointing to me? People often give a description of you as 'She is anointed' or 'She is an anointed singer.' Can you tell me exactly what that is and what it means to be anointed?" I moaned, grunted, and spoke some things that sounded spiritual, but my words really didn't have any depth or meaning. After that little encounter I was determined that I was going to find out what this "possession" was that I had in my grasp and what it was truly capable of. I set out on a journey to try and put my arms around this thing called "the anointing."

I believe with everything inside of me that God wants each of His children to walk in the anointing and giftings He has destined for our lives. I also believe He wants to impart a "fresh anointing" on you as you read this book, one that will change your life forever. I pray you will say as David said in Psalm 92:10, "You [Lord] have made me as strong as a wild ox. You have anointed me with the finest oil" (NLT).

The anointing is so simply powerful yet uniquely profound. There are many definitions we could use to try and capture what it is. Matter-of-factly I have made it my business to collect testimonials from as many powerful men and women of God that the Lord is speaking to and through today to help me try to define this gift from the Holy Spirit that has been given to us. You will find them peppered throughout the book as you read, and you'll also learn that while these testimonials sound similar, they are very different. That's because the anointing means something different to each individual, yet it is the same to everyone.

The anointing is something the Father gives that is distinctly ours and ours alone, yet it is the same Holy Spirit who endows all of God's children with this phenomenal gift. What a paradox! So before we examine some examples of demonstrating the anointing, let's go back in the Word again to begin defining it.

THE PURPOSE OF THE ANOINTING

So, what is the anointing? What is its purpose? Generally speaking, the anointing is the power of God to accomplish His purposes, regardless of the sphere of your ministry. My husband, Pastor Jamie Tuttle, says this about the anointing: "The anointing is simply the fuel of God's presence on one for the purpose of the establishment of God's kingdom. It is what some call *unction*, and it precedes supernatural manifestation and demonstration of God through His people."[1]

The first mention of the word *anointing* is found in Exodus 25, and it is used in the context of preparing an offering for the first tabernacle in the wilderness.

> And the Lord said to Moses, Speak to the Israelites, that they take for Me an offering. From every man who gives it willingly and ungrudgingly with his heart you shall take My offering. This is the offering you shall receive from them: gold, silver, and bronze, blue, purple, and scarlet...and fine twined linen and goats' hair, rams' skins tanned red, goatskins, dolphin or porpoise skins, acacia wood, oil for the light, spices for anointing oil and for sweet incense, onyx stones, and stones for setting in the ephod and in the breastplate. Let them make Me a sanctuary, that I may dwell among them. And you shall make it according to all that I show you, the pattern of the tabernacle or dwelling and the pattern of all the furniture of it.
> —Exodus 25:1–9, AMP, EMPHASIS ADDED

I want you to notice that the anointing is first mentioned in preparation for the tabernacle of God, the place that would eventually house the presence of God. Also notice that the spices for the anointing oil and sweet incense came as an offering to the Lord. Both the tabernacle and the spices for the anointing oil are Old Testament patterns, "types and shadows" if you will, that are fulfilled in the New Testament. We'll get to this shortly.

One thing to grab hold of now is that when God mentions a concept or idea for the first time in the Scriptures, as He has concerning the anointing, it usually means He is setting up an archetype! "Wow," you might say, "What is that? It sounds all fancy." According to Webster's the word *archetype* means "the original pattern or model of which all things of the same type are representations or copies,"[2] or in other words, "the original, the prime example, or the very best on display."

THE ORIGINAL ESSENCE OF THE ANOINTING

Now let's look at the meaning of the anointing, and then capture the original essence of what it's all about. The Hebrew word for "anoint" is *māshaḥ* (pronounced maw-shakh'). It means "to rub with oil; i.e., to anoint; by implication to consecrate; also to paint."[3] The Hebrew word for "anointing" is *mishḥâ* (pronounced meesh-khaw'), which comes from the root word *anoint*, and means an "unction (the act); by implication a consecratory gift."[4] The Old Testament generally speaks of "anointing" in the sense of a special setting apart for an office or function.[5]

The "anointing oil" mentioned in Exodus 25:6 was made up of very special ingredients. Obviously there is no way to fully exhaust the subject matter about this oil, but here is what I found the anointing oil was made up of based on Exodus 30:22–25:

- Pure myrrh: This is the resin from a small, thorny tree collected when one wounds the tree by penetrating the bark.

  Get ready. If you are going to flow in the anointing, you better be prepared to be wounded and penetrated. God will never use anyone unless He tests them first, so get ready for some testing. Jesus said, "In the world you will have tribulation; but be of good cheer, I have overcome the world."

  Paul said in 2 Corinthians 4:7, "We have this treasure in earthen vessels, that the excellency of the power may be of God, and not of us" (KJV). That means we are dirt, but the treasure is in the dirt, and that means it is within us.

  Jeremiah 12:5 declares, "If you have run with the footmen, and they have wearied you, then how can you contend with horses?" Every day we will have to contend for the faith and sometimes that means being wounded.

- Sweet cinnamon: This spice comes from islands in the Indian Ocean. It is produced from the dried inner rind of the tree.

- Sweet calamus: This is a fragrant cane whose root is highly prized as a spice. It grows in Arabia and India.

   Sometimes we will go through dry seasons, but dry seasons don't last forever.

   If you find someone who is genuinely anointed by God and walking in that anointing and gifting every day, you are going to find a "sweet" person. I don't know about you, but I don't like being around mean people, especially if they claim the name of Jesus. But there are some who do, and they are the worst kind. In 1 Corinthians 13 Paul basically said in "…tongues will cease, prophecies will cease, but love lasts forever."

- Cassia: This is the aromatic bark of a shrub resembling the cinnamon tree.

   Cassia is very hard on the outside. God told the prophets, "Don't be afraid of their faces…" (Jer. 1:8) and to set their faces like flint (Ezek. 3:9). Flint is the hardest of rocks. There is no room for fragility in this army. Matthew 11:12 states that "the kingdom of heaven suffers violence, and the violent take it by force." At times the anointing will require some thick-skinned people of God who have zeal and grit all at the same time. Also remember God is looking for "dead people." You can't hurt a dead person with your words, the way you look at them or the way you treat them. Paul said, "I have been crucified with Christ; it is no longer I who live, but Christ lives in me" (Gal. 2:20).

- Pure olive oil: Olive oil "is supposed to be the best preservative of odours."[6] Wine, olive oil, and bread are the three main staples of Israel and this list is repeated throughout the Old Testament.

  The anointing will make you look good. The Bible says that God will "beautify the meek with salvation" (Ps. 146:4, KJV). With salvation comes an anointing. This same anointing will also preserve and keep your heart and your mind.

  The anointing will make you smell good. Everybody wants to be around someone who smells good. That could be in the natural or the supernatural.

  The anointing will preserve you. It preserves your life, your walk, your testimony, your integrity, and your character. It will keep you through the thick and the thin, the ups and the downs, and in sickness and in health, which means when the devil hits you, you can keep on ticking and kicking every day. You not only talk the talk, but you also walk the walk.

- Stacte: The gum of the storax tree found in the East.

  This is a sticky substance that holds the oil together. If we are going to make it, we have to stick together as the body of Christ. We cannot make it without each other. There is an impartation that comes from each one of our anointings. We need our worship leader's anointing to take us into an atmosphere of worship. We need a prophetic word or revelation to come from our pastors, prophets, and teachers. We need to be around each other.

One thing I know is that on a Sunday morning, a television or computer will not put their arms around you and hug you like a brother or sister in the Lord will when you need encouragement. That's why it is important for us to stick together.

When you are anointed, you have to be able to hold things together with your confession of faith. The Word says, "Faith comes by hearing, and hearing by the word of God" (Rom. 10:17). You can't be up one day and down the next; living in faith one minute and fear, doubt, and unbelief the next minute. The Word says, "Be doers of the word, and not a hearers only" (James 1:22). James says "a double-minded man [is], unstable in all his ways" (James 1:8). The bottom line, "the just shall *live* by faith" (Gal. 3:11, emphasis added).

- Onycha: It comes from a sweet-smelling shell found on the shores of the Red Sea and the Indian Ocean; it also increases the smell of other perfumes.

- Galbanum: It is the juice of a shrub growing in Arabia.

  With the anointing on your life, you automatically carry a smell, an aroma, or a fragrance that will draw others to you and you will see a great harvest of souls coming into the kingdom. Also you will find yourself being hooked up with people of like-faith, like-spirit, like-destiny, and like-anointing.

- Pure frankincense: This is the most important of the aromatic gums and is regarded by itself as a precious perfume.

  The most important thing as you are pursuing this

anointing on your life will be for you to understand that this special presence of God is something that is of great worth and most precious. Something that I have tried to do all my life is to guard this anointing. As the great King Solomon counseled, "Guard your heart above all else, for it is the source of life" (HCSB).

Paul said, "Do you not know that you are the temple of God and that the Spirit of God dwells in you? If anyone defiles the temple of God, God will destroy him. For the temple of God is holy, which temple you are" (1 Cor. 3:16–17).

All of these ingredients were ordained and commissioned by God and were exactly what He demanded to go into the oil that would be used to consecrate the tabernacle, the ark, the table of show-bread, the brazen altar, and all their utensils. The holy anointing oil was also used to consecrate Aaron and his sons to minister to God as priests (Exod. 30:26–30). In essence, God was saying to Moses, "Anything that has to do with My work and the work of My kingdom has to be special, set apart, sanctified, and holy. It must be extraordinary and unique in My own way. And this is exactly how I want it to be done."

God always has been and always will be a God of specifics. If you don't believe me, talk to Noah about the ark. Then have a good talk with Moses about the tabernacle and all the different laws and precepts that the children of Israel were instructed to observe (which many of them, especially Orthodox Jews, still observe to this day).

After this, if you still want to talk specifics, take a close look at Leviticus and Numbers. Both of these foundational books, along with the other three books of Moses, have details that put baseball specs to shame. "According to the pattern" is a term used over and over again in Scripture because God made sure to establish solid archetypes under the old covenant that He would fulfill in the new.

THE FULLNESS OF THE ANOINTING

What God did throughout thousands of years of Jewish history was pointing to a future when He would fulfill the Old Testament tabernacle with the New Testament temple, and the holy anointing oil with the gifts presented in worship to Jesus shortly after His birth. When the three wise men from the East brought gold, frankincense and myrrh to Jesus (Matt. 2:1–11), the prophetic was at work, foretelling amazing things that would come to pass.

- Gold: Considered very valuable, gold was a symbol of kingship on the earth.

- Frankincense: This gummy substance wasn't in the original holy anointing oil, and it needs no help from those ingredients. It represents Jesus's life and sacrificial death as a sweet-smelling aroma to Father God.[7]

- Myrrh: This resin was part of the original anointing oil and is a prophetic representation of the wounding of the Lord Jesus. The prophet Isaiah spoke about the Anointed One and said, "He was wounded for our transgressions, He was bruised for our iniquities; the chastisement of our peace was upon Him, and by His stripes we are healed" (Isa. 53:5).

Now, let's keep digging and revisit the Hebrew word for "anointing": *mishḥâ*. When you look deeper, you will discover this word is related to the original word *māshîaḥ* (pronounced maw-shee-akh'), the "anointed one," from which the term "messiah" comes. You will also find that the New Testament title of Christ is derived from the Greek *Christos,* which is equivalent of *māshîaḥ.* Both words are rooted in the idea of "to smear with oil."[8] Amen! God put a firm foundation in place to fulfill His anointing.

So how does this tie in with the New Testament temple?

Remember that the ingredients for the holy anointing oil were among the *first things* God called for in the *first offering* to establish the Old Testament tabernacle in Exodus 25:1–9. Everything in the tabernacle, as well as the brazen altar in the outer court where burnt sacrifices were made daily, was anointed with that most holy oil. Even the priests were smeared with the oil of that anointing, which foretold the perfect priesthood of Jesus Christ.

When Jesus said, "Destroy this temple, and in three days I will raise it up" (John 2:19), He wasn't talking about the tabernacle in Jerusalem. He was declaring His body would be raised to life in three days by the power of the anointing. The Old Testament burnt offerings, grain offerings, and peace offerings that God had broken down to Moses in Leviticus 1–7 have now been fulfilled with one *final* offering:

> God's will was for us to be made holy by the sacrifice of the body of Jesus Christ, once for all time. Under the old covenant, the priest stands and ministers before the altar day after day, offering the same sacrifices again and again, which can never take away sins. But our High Priest offered himself to God as a single sacrifice for sins, good for all time. Then he sat down in the place of honor at God's right hand. There he waits until his enemies are humbled and made a footstool under his feet. For by that one offering he forever made perfect those who are being made holy.
>
> —HEBREWS 10:10–14, NLT

I love that! God's only begotten Son, Jesus, declared He had made the final and complete sacrifice when He hung His head and cried, "It is finished!" (See John 19:30.) The portable tabernacle in the wilderness, which the Israelites had to set up and break down every time they moved camp, was ultimately fulfilled by Jesus Christ Himself.

And it gets even better. The apostle Paul later expanded the New Testament theme of the spiritual temple to include the church. He said:

> Do you not know that you are the temple of God and that the Spirit of God dwells in you? If anyone defiles the temple of God, God will destroy him. For the temple of God is holy, which temple you are.
> —1 Corinthians 3:16–17, emphasis added

So when we consider how Jesus operated in and fulfilled the original archetypes of the anointing set up in Scripture, what does all of this tell us? The anointing is always connected to one of two things:

1. What God is doing in us

2. What God is doing through us

In turn, we will give all the glory right back to Him. Always remember as you grow in the anointing: everything that God has ever created is for His purpose and glory.

The Anointing Purifies You for God's Purpose

The anointing that comes from God brings results. There will be no growth in your walk with God without His anointing operating in your life. When His anointing comes upon you, you will immediately begin to experience many changes. You will begin to experience miracles, signs, and wonders in your life. Miracles are divine supernatural interventions in the natural affairs of man. It is when everybody has done everything in the natural and nothing has worked, and it is then that God steps in through the supernatural to do that which only God can do.

The anointing will cause you to have a change in purpose and changes in your heart, mind, and actions. You will no longer have any sense that you are able to bring radical change to your life, and certainly not to anyone else's life, without total submission to God.

The truth of the matter is, the Lord wants ALL of you: nothing more, nothing less. Period. This can be hard to comprehend, but remember that even Jesus had to *learn obedience* when He walked on the earth. Because He completed His mission, you are anointed to stay the course. One thing I have learned about this journey and pursuit of living out God's purpose is that *His purpose shall stand.*

Think about the spices in the holy anointing oil. They had to be scraped, ground, bled, burned, and so on in order to be pure and holy, ready for His intended use. Just as He instructed this to be done to these holy spices, believe me, He will do that to you when He gets ready to use you. Everything that can be shaken has to be removed so those things that can't be shaken will remain.

When I left my home in North Carolina, I left everything that was familiar to me—everything that I loved, the places that said *home* to me, the people whom I loved and who loved me—only to be challenged to live in totally unfamiliar surroundings, not knowing who would be my friends and family in my new home away from home. In doing so, I was in essence saying to God, "This is all of me, God. Take me." And take me He did. I have never looked back. That was thirty-three years ago.

As I said earlier in this chapter, the anointing manifests in many wonderful ways, but in its purest sense I have learned it is the power that furnishes whatever you need in order to accomplish your unique purpose in the kingdom of God.

When I look back on the faithfulness of God, it is really astounding to realize how His hand has kept me, protected me, and allowed me to see countless lives changed, all because I said yes to His chosen will for my life. Looking back, I understand that I had to overcome many obstacles, including loneliness, the loss of both my mom and dad while I was away, and more. As I walked by faith and obeyed God, He was purifying me, because He was anointing me to fulfill His purpose.

God demands pure vessels. The Old Testament tabernacle has so many types and shadows for us to learn, grasp, and walk out in our everyday lives. I love to study the tabernacle because every time that I do, I learn something new. Recently as I was studying I came across the words of Bill Bright, the founder of Campus Crusade for Christ:

> The reason the laver was polished so finely was to reflect the image of the person standing in front of it, the person who came to wash his hands and feet. This is a picture of examining ourselves with the help of the Holy Spirit and confessing any sin we find. The Bible tells us, "If we confess our sins to Him, He is faithful and just to forgive us and to cleanse us from every wrong..." (1 John 1:9–10).[9]

First John 3:3 plainly tells us, "And everyone who had this hope in Him purifies himself, just as He is pure." One pastor has stated, "In the Greek, the verb is *hagnizei eauton,* which is a present active indicative, meaning, 'he purifies himself daily, continually, moment by moment.'"[10]

Wow! What is "this hope"? It is the second appearing of our Lord and Savior, Jesus Christ. So, if you believe that Jesus's return to the earth could happen at any moment, by the power of the anointing you are purifying yourself daily. The Holy Spirit, the keeper of the anointing and our comforter and teacher, helps us to purify ourselves. He is getting the bride of Christ ready for that great day when we will be united with our Beloved. He promised that He would lead and guide us into all truth. The Holy Spirit is there as the keeper of the anointing to protect, remind, convict, and draw you into Jesus and into a greater anointing with Him.

TRUE LIFE EXAMPLES OF OPERATING IN THE ANOINTING

Now, how is the anointing demonstrated? The Bible is full of godly men and women whose lives demonstrated the anointing God had entrusted to them. Their examples are there for us so that we can be reminded of the faithfulness of the Father and what Jesus has promised: "He who believes in Me, the works that I do he will do also; and greater works than these he will do, because I go to My Father" (John 14:12).

First of all, let's look at Abraham, the father of many nations (Gen. 17:1–5). God told him, "Take now your son, your only son Isaac, whom you love, and go to the land of Moriah, and offer him there as a burnt offering on one of the mountains of which I shall tell you" (Gen. 22:2).

One thing that has always seemed so interesting to me is how the Bible says, "So Abraham *rose early* in the morning" and got going (v. 3, emphasis added). I can't imagine how Abraham felt as he got up and prepared to do what God had told him. I don't know, I might have waited until at least around midday to see if God might change His mind. Not Abraham! He was determined to obey God and flow in the leading of His Spirit, power, and anointing.

The true picture of the anointing in this story is Abraham raising that knife upward and getting ready to slay his son as a sacrifice to God. He was so bent on obeying God that the angel of the Lord had to call out his name twice to stop him (vv. 10–11). Abraham was anointed to obey God, even to the point of killing his only son, because the Bible says he was convinced that God would absolutely raise Isaac from the dead. (See Hebrews 11:17–19.) Of course, this encounter is a type and shadow of what Father God did for us by giving us His one and only Son to die for our sins.

Then there is Moses, a man who talked to God face-to-face (Num. 12:6–8). This wasn't so at the beginning of his life, but something happened in the wilderness when he saw the burning bush (Exod. 3:2). All of a sudden he was struck with his purpose and identity; he received an anointing that was so strong he was able to stand before the great pharaoh of Egypt and boldly proclaim, "Thus says the LORD God of Israel, 'Let My people go...'" (Exod. 5:1).

This is the same Moses who ran away from Pharaoh after he had killed an Egyptian, fearing for his life (Exod. 2:11–15). But by the power of the anointing he later stood in front of him as a seasoned man of God and declared the word of the Lord concerning the people of Israel.

One of our favorite stories to preach about and read to our children is the story of David and Goliath (1 Sam. 17). There is no other story in the Bible that is so exciting. Every time I read this account of young David, I get a vivid visual of exactly what happened and what this scene must have looked like.

Can you imagine this ruddy kid coming against something as mammoth as a giant? David was so offended by the way Goliath was making fun of the God of Israel that he was determined to do something to shut his mouth. The Bible says that David declared, "Who is this uncircumcised Philistine, that he should defy the armies of the living God?" (v. 26). Then when he headed to the battle, David picked up five smooth stones from the river, and when he started to run toward Goliath to take him out, he took out one of those stones, under the anointing of God, and slung it toward the giant.

Not only did he hit him in the "sweet spot" so the stone sank into his forehead, but when Goliath fell, David took Goliath's own sword and cut his head off. (See 1 Samuel 17:26–51.) He was truly anointed for that mighty work! (Whoa! I can preach right here!) That is exactly what you are about to do with this anointing that is coming upon you. God is going to give you the power and boldness to take the heads off of giants of fear, doubt, and unbelief. And you're going to take up the sword of the Spirit, which is the Word of God and slay with the anointing every enemy of God that is coming against your life. And believe me, when they fall, they won't get back up again.

A New Testament example is John the Baptist, who preached out in the desert and thousands came to be baptized by him, including Jesus, the Anointed One (Matt. 3:1–6, 13–15). John wasn't intimidated by the religious leaders of the day. When they came to him in the wilderness, his response to them was, "'You brood of snakes!' he exclaimed. 'Who warned you to flee God's coming wrath? Prove by the way you live that you have repented of your sins and turned to God. Don't just say to each other, "We're safe, for we are descendants of Abraham." That means nothing, for I tell you, God can create children of Abraham from these very stones'" (vv. 7–9, NLT).

Each of these men knew God and understood the anointing intimately, because they protected it. They operated and functioned in God's anointing as the Spirit led them, and they walked in true repentance, holiness, and the fear of the Lord. The anointing on our lives can't be used to its fullest potential unless we live consecrated, dedicated, sanctified, and set-apart lives for the glory of Almighty God.

As I have already shown you, Jesus Christ, the Anointed One, is the ultimate example of demonstrating the anointing. In Acts 10:38 Peter expounded: "God anointed Jesus of Nazareth with the Holy Spirit and with *power*, who went about doing good and healing all who were oppressed by the devil, for God was with Him" (emphasis added).

When Mary (Martha's sister) "took a pound of very costly oil of spikenard, anointed the feet of Jesus, and wiped His feet with her hair…," Judas called it a *waste,* but the Lord received it as *worship*

(John 12:3–8). Jesus told him, "Let her alone; she has kept this for the day of my burial" (v. 7).

Jesus was the ultimate sacrifice, the Lamb of God who was slain before the foundation of the world. He is our perfect High Priest who gave His life once for all, "who is seated at the right hand of the throne of the Majesty in the heavens, a Minister of the sanctuary and of the true tabernacle which the Lord erected, and not man" (Heb. 8:1–2).

Hallelujah! Jesus did all of the work, paid the highest price, and fulfilled the original archetype of the anointing. When He cried out from the cross, "It is finished," everything we needed to know about God and to walk in His anointing was abundantly provided. Hebrews 9:13–14 says, "For if the blood of bulls and goats and the ashes of a heifer, sprinkling the unclean, sanctifies for the purifying of the flesh, how much more shall the blood of Christ, who through the eternal Spirit offered Himself without spot to God, cleanse your conscience from dead works to serve the living God?"

Are we perfect? No! But Jesus is! When we come to Him and confess our sins, He forgives and cleanses us from all unrighteousness. By the power of the Holy Spirit, the keeper of the anointing, we can "cleanse ourselves" and depart from iniquity so we become pure vessels fit for the Master's use (2 Tim. 2:21). We have a surety of a better covenant through Jesus Christ. By His suffering He has perfected forever those who are sanctified; that's you and me!

Now I declare to you: there are many expressions of the anointing, but Jesus is the very definition and the demonstration of it! He not only knew what the anointing was, but He also embodied the anointing and functioned in it—perfectly—every day of His life. Why? He knew His purpose in coming to earth as a human being. He stayed the course and fulfilled every prophetic promise concerning Himself as the Anointed One.

Yet Jesus did not leave us as orphans when He was raised from the dead and returned to heaven to sit at the right hand of the Father. He promised, "I will pray the Father, and He will give you another Helper, that He may abide with you forever—the Spirit of truth, whom the world cannot receive, because it neither sees Him nor knows Him; but you know Him, for He dwells with you and will be in you" (John 14:16–17).

Friend, this promise is for you, and the same anointing abides within you. I declare in agreement with the Word of God that you will receive and operate in the fullness of the anointing. You will do greater works! Why? The Spirit of the Lord is upon you! *You are anointed for this!*

∞ LET IT BE to ME . . .

Life is full of paradoxes, especially when the anointing comes into a situation and begins turning it around for the glory of God. *Have you been confused about the anointing, maybe even afraid of it at times? Are you prepared to fulfill God's destined purpose for your life?* Now that you understand the purpose of the anointing, have seen the Old Testament types and shadows of its original essence, and know that Jesus Christ has released the anointing in all its fullness—it's time to take advantage of this heavenly gift.

From what you've read up to this point, you know the anointing comes to us through the power of the Holy Spirit. *Are you intimately acquainted with Him?* If not, say yes to God, step out into new, unfamiliar territory, and never look back!

I agree with you now, in the mighty name of Jesus, that you will be filled to overflowing with the fullness of the Holy Spirit and that tangible evidence of the Lord's anointing will follow you wherever you go all the days of your life. I declare, "Let it be to you according to the Word of God"... *because you are anointed for this!*

three

YOU ARE ANOINTED *for* THIS

*"Go therefore and make disciples of all the nations, baptizing them
in the name of the Father and of the Son and of the Holy Spirit,
teaching them to observe all things that I have commanded you;
and lo, I am with you always, even to the end of the age." Amen.*

—MATTHEW 28:19–20

TODAY AS I walk in God's purpose, I find myself in Lagos, Nigeria, in the heart of the city at the Tafawa Balewa Square. It is here that the entire commerce of the city is located, and it is where Nigeria's Independence Celebration took place on October 1, 1960. Here the namesake of the square, Prime Minister Tafawa Balewa, delivered his independence speech that set this nation on a different course. The entrance to the square has four giant white horses suspended above the gate and seven red eagles. These are the symbols from the national emblem, signifying strength and dignity, respectively.[1]

Tafawa Balewa Square is also the place where more than 600,000 people are coming together for twelve hours of nonstop praise and worship to Jesus Christ, our King. The air is very warm, and nighttime has already fallen over this city of over 13 million people of different backgrounds, languages, and financial statuses—but one thing we all have in common is that we're all part of the family of

God. Believe me, if you could see what I see at this moment, God has a very large family. There is a sea of people as far as the eye can see.

Many well-known artists have arrived on this soil to proclaim that Nigeria belongs to Jesus and to take part in one of the largest praise and worship concerts known in Christendom. As we arrive in our security-escorted vehicles, we drive very slowly as we approach the people-infested area where "The Experience" will take place. We make our way into the venue where the worship is already taking place and the atmosphere is charged with the anointing of the Holy Spirit. Hundreds of thousands are entering into a time of exaltation and worship.

Our hostess comfortably seats us in an area reserved for us as we wait and collect our thoughts, prepare, and pray for ourselves and those who are onstage already. We have come to Lagos with high expectations that lives would be radically changed forever. As I'm sitting there, I suddenly realize the mammoth task that is ahead of me. Getting up in front of 600,000 plus people isn't something that I do every weekend. So I find myself feeling more and more comfortable standing and walking, as I love to do when I pray.

As I begin to walk, I think to myself, "I'm just going to take this time to pray and get into the worship that is happening onstage and across these fields of thousands giving worship to God." All of a sudden the reality of what is about to happen in my life surfaces so quickly that it literally takes my breath away. Seemingly out of nowhere feelings of anxiety, intimidation, and inadequacy begin to invade my mind, and the stark realization that I am about to minister to over half a million people is totally overwhelming. (And literally, that figure does not include the millions and even billions who are participating by satellite.) But the satellite thing isn't concerning me as much as the hundreds of thousands who are directly in front of me; that is absolutely getting my attention.

The more I pray, the more it feels as if the enemy is gaining a foothold with thoughts in my mind. "What if I forget the words? What if I fall down the steps going on the stage with all the huge screens? What if...? What if...?" So I begin to combat these feelings and emotions, turning them into thoughts of what the Word says about me. Remember, the Word is our final authority! We look to the Word to see what it says about our situation when we feel we have come up against the impossible.

The first thing that comes to my mind is this book that I'm already working on, *You Are Anointed for This!* As I'm pacing back and forth, I begin to say this to myself, "I am anointed for this! I am anointed for this!" Then I walk over to pull the curtain back, and my eyes confirm what I feel in the pit of my stomach: "Oh, my goodness. I've never seen so many people in my life in one place." I keep pacing and praying. I have brought two background singers with me, so I walk over to them and through my anxiety am trying to encourage them, when, in my mind, they need to be encouraging me. I say to Chris and Regenna, "Listen, guys, we are anointed for this. Let's just declare that together: 'We are anointed for this. We are anointed for this!'" The more we say it, the more we believe it. Sometimes you just have to talk to yourself to get the mind of God in your situation.

You, *Yes*, *You*, Are Anointed!

What you must understand is that the devil doesn't want you to know you are anointed. He knows that as a child of God you are called to go whenever and wherever God sends you to do His kingdom work. So the enemy wants to make you believe that you are defeated, that you are less than adequate. For example, he would come to me and say, "Grammy Award winner Israel Houghton may be anointed for 600,000; Mary Mary may be anointed for 600,000; Don Moen or Fred Hammond may be...but not Judy Jacobs. You're just a little ol' Native American girl, the youngest of twelve children from North Carolina. Not you!" The enemy's goal is for me to believe his lies, so I'd say, "Wow! You're right, devil. Not me."

This reminds me of the story of Gideon in the Book of Judges. During a time when the Israelites were being oppressed by their enemies, the angel of the Lord visited Gideon and told him, "The LORD is with you, you mighty man of valor!...Go in this might of yours, and you shall save Israel from the hand of the Midianites" (Judg. 6:12, 14). Gideon said, "Who me? I am the least among my people" (v. 15, author's paraphrase). God didn't let Gideon off the hook, He didn't let me off the hook in Lagos, and He's not going to let you off the hook either. *You are anointed for this.* Whatever your *this* is, whatever God is calling you to do, He says you are anointed for it.

Quite frankly I felt like Gideon. It seemed as if everybody had brought their four- and five-piece bands, their three and four background vocalists, and a choir to back them up. Me? It was just two backup singers, my tracks, and me on a stage that was the size of a football field, or so it seemed, and more than 600,000 screaming Nigerian brothers and sisters, who are known for their exuberant worship, ready to jump, shout, dance, and "make a joyful noise."

God told Gideon in Judges 7:2–3, "You have too many warriors with you; send some of them home" (author's paraphrase). Gideon must have thought, "You know, Lord, that is really funny. But can we get serious here? I mean, look at the size of our enemy." If Gideon had said that to God, He would have simply told him, "I AM serious; you have too many people!" But Gideon did what God told him to do. Gideon looked at the people and said, "Anyone who is fearful, go home!" The Bible says, "Twenty-two thousand of the people returned, and ten thousand remained" (v. 3).

Why did God cut back on the number of warriors who would go to battle with Gideon? He told Gideon very clearly: "Lest Israel claim glory for itself against Me, saying, 'My own hands have saved me'" (v. 2). God doesn't want three quarters, half, or just a little bit of the glory. He wants *all* the glory. He declares, "I, the LORD your God, am a jealous God" (Exod. 20:5). God will not share His glory with anyone.

Then God said something to Gideon that was totally unbelievable. Allow me to paraphrase: "Uh, hey, listen, Gideon. I hate to tell you this, but you still have too many." I'm sure by this point Gideon had to be feeling, "OK, God, I am going to pull all of my hair out." The Bible says that God told him, "Bring them down to the water, and I will test them for you there" (Judg. 7:4).

God reduced the number of Gideon's warriors to three hundred men, "those who lapped [from the water], putting their hand to their mouth" (v. 6). That puny, little army of three hundred warriors that Gideon had left faced a multitude. Can you imagine preparing to fight an army the Bible describes as being "as numerous as locusts; and their camels were without number, as the sand by the seashore in multitude" (v. 12)? Maybe not, but can you remember a time when God told you to do something that seemed overwhelming? I declare to you: God is able.

YOU CAN PASS THE TEST

Did you know that God will never use anyone unless He tests them first? So if you feel like you're "all that and a bag of chips," I want to warn you: get ready for some testing. The Bible says, "In a great house there are not only vessels of gold and silver, but also of wood and clay, some for honor and some for dishonor. Therefore if anyone cleanses himself from the latter, he will be a vessel for honor, sanctified and useful for the Master, prepared for every good work" (2 Tim. 2:20–21).

You may remember I mentioned this verse toward the end of the last chapter. So let me ask you—did you get that word *prepared*?

Remember, it is through His anointing that God purifies you to fulfill His purpose. That's why God will test you before He uses you. He'll tell you to do something and then expect you to do it. That's how, by the power of the Holy Spirit, you can *cleanse yourself*. God tested Gideon's warriors on the riverside. Those whose hearts were the most prepared to trust Him, and Gideon, in battle received the anointing to go and fulfill His purpose.

When God is getting ready to use you, whether it's on a small or large scale, *there will be some preparation*. The word *prepare* means, "to put in proper condition or readiness."[2] When God calls you to do a work for Him, you have to communicate to your flesh, "Something is getting ready to happen." Then your spirit has to come into agreement that *this is your time, your turn, your season to be anointed for whatever God has put you on this planet for.*

You might feel as if you are the most insignificant person there is, but you have to—on purpose—change your mind about yourself. Transformation begins, first of all, in your thoughts, exactly as it did with Gideon. That's why God declared to Gideon, "You mighty man of valor!", while he was hiding wheat from the Midianites in a winepress (Judg. 6:11–12). That's why, as I was pressing in to the Word before going onstage in Lagos, Nigeria, the Holy Spirit brought this book to my mind—so I would declare, "I am anointed for this!", and do what He called me to do in that place.

There has to be a metamorphosis that transforms caterpillar thinking to the next level: to the anointing of a butterfly, or even better, an eagle. This kind of transformation is only found in the anointing of God and by allowing the Holy Spirit to change us from the inside out as we do what God tells us to do.

Dr. Martin Luther King Jr. once told the story of riding the bus across town every day to attend high school. In those days blacks were required to sit at the back of the bus while whites sat in the front. Even if there weren't any white people on the bus, blacks still could not sit in the front. If all the "black" seats were occupied, riders had to stand over empty seats that were reserved for whites.

"I would end up having to go to the back of the bus with my body," said Dr. King, "but every time I got on that bus I left my mind up on the front seat. And I said to myself, 'One of these days, I'm going to put my body up there where my mind is.'"[3] God anointed him for that! And the world knows that Dr. King went on to do many mighty works for God. As a man thinks in his heart, so is he (Prov. 23:7).

WHAT HAS GOD ANOINTED YOU TO DO?

Now what about you? Are you prepared to obey God and start (or keep) moving in your purpose, no matter how overwhelming it may seem to be? If you're ready to say yes to God, it's time to take on a new mind-set. The Word of God says, "Don't let the world around you squeeze you into its own mould, but let God re-mould your minds from within" (Rom. 12:2, PHILLIPS). Paul continues in the same verse, "Then you will learn to know God's will for you, which is good and pleasing and perfect" (NLT)

I love the way *The Message* translates Romans 12:1–2:

> So here's what I want you to do, God helping you: Take your everyday, ordinary life—your sleeping, eating, going-to-work, and walking-around life—and place it before God as an offering.... Don't become so well-adjusted to your culture that you fit into it without even thinking. Instead, fix your attention on God. You'll be changed from the inside out. Readily recognize what he wants from you, and quickly respond to it. Unlike the culture around you, always dragging you down to its level of immaturity, God brings the best out of you, develops well-formed maturity in you.

What is it that God has called and anointed you to do? What specific things is He expecting from you as you answer His call to go and make disciples? Don't adjust your life and ministry to the limitations of the world's culture around you. God has called you to believe Him and stand out to make a difference in this world by embracing your calling. Read the words of Amanda Fisher, a dynamic young revivalist and reconciliation minister, with me. As you read, I pray the Lord will reveal or confirm to you the anointing He has placed upon your life.

> The anointing sets you apart for a specific task. It is what God has placed on you and in you and should be guarded by how you live your life. It is a continual flow that does not run out; it cannot be exhausted. The anointing goes beyond what man can accomplish and deflects the evil one.
>
> God has always placed importance on the anointing. In Exodus we see that in order to minister to God, priests had to be anointed. When Jesus was on the earth, He was anointed for burial by a woman pouring out her love. The disciples were anointed as Christ transformed them into His likeness, and we, as sons and daughters of God, like Jesus, are anointed "...to preach the good news (the Gospel) to the poor..." He has sent us "...to announce release to the captives and recovery of sight to the blind, to send forth as delivered those who are oppressed..." (Luke 4:18, AMP). We are sent to proclaim the favorable year of the Lord.
>
> There is a strong connection between the anointing and being filled with the power of the Holy Spirit. Just as in the Old Testament God anointed the priests to set them apart to minister to Himself, He anoints His people today and empowers them through the Holy Spirit. A definition of *anointing* in the original Greek is "enduing Christians with the gifts of the Holy Spirit." The anointing is the forthright

commissioning that is carried out by the explosive power of the Holy Spirit. By staying sensitive to the working of the Holy Spirit in our lives, we can grow and operate in the specific anointing for our lives. We must not forsake the necessity of the power of the Holy Spirit operating actively through us. It is this power that enables us to resist the enemy and fulfill our anointed call.[4]

Amen! That's how Gideon rose up and became a deliverer in Israel—through the mighty anointing of God. In the eyes of the Lord the anointing is an invaluable resource in our lives. Without it we can't do anything of eternal value. But remember what Jesus said: "…with God all things are possible" (Matt. 19:26). You can rise up, tap in to God and His inexhaustible flow of the anointing, and fulfill what He has called you to do in this life. You are anointed for victory!

Now, you might be saying, "Judy, how did you do in Lagos, Nigeria?" Well, let me tell you, the power of God was so strong and the anointing flowed so richly that people were worshipping and praising God on their feet practically the whole time. His presence and anointing made all the difference as more than 600,000 people were shouting, jumping, screaming, blowing whistles, and clapping their hands before Him. Some were just lifting their hands in worship and praise to Father God, but I'll tell you this without hesitation: His will and purpose were accomplished that day.

DECLARE AND EMBRACE THE ANOINTING!

Right now, as you consider your calling and continue to pour over this book and the revelation that I know you are receiving, it's important to declare these things aloud so that they will be established in your life. I love this declarative prayer by my friend Cindy Trimm. She is very experienced in decreeing a thing and seeing it come to pass. I encourage you to bookmark this page and declare these statements every day if you can, to establish your place in the anointing and in the kingdom of God.

> *All powerful God, place the following anointings upon me, and let them flow uncontaminated and unhindered in my life:*
>
> - *Solomon's anointing for resource management, wisdom, wealth, success, and prosperity*
>
> - *Issac's anointing for investment strategies*
>
> - *Cyrus's anointing for financial acumen*
>
> - *Samuel's anointing for sensitivity and obedience to the voice of God*
>
> - *Esther's anointing for divine favor and kingdom strategies*
>
> - *Daniel's anointing for government, excellence, and integrity*
>
> - *Joseph's anointing for political, business, and economic leadership strategies*
>
> - *Joshua's anointing for warfare, prosperity, and success strategies*
>
> - *Abraham's anointing for pioneering new territories, real estate acquisitions, and intergenerational covenant blessings*
>
> - *Moses's anointing as a trailblazer and leader*
>
> - *Nehemiah's anointing as a renovator and restorer*

- *Ezra's anointing as an authentic worshipper of the true and living God*

- *Deborah's anointing for balance*

- *David's anointing for worship and praise*

- *Paul's anointing for cutting-edge apostolic revelation*

- *Elijah's anointing for prophetic accuracy and insights*

- *Elisha's anointing for servanthood, ministerial succession, and the double portion of jurisdictional power and authority*

- *Issachar's anointing for the discernment of correct times and seasons*

- *Abigail's anointing for hospitality and prudence*

- *Anna's anointing for intercession*

- *Christ's anointing for prophetic prayer, spiritual warfare, signs, wonders, miracles, and a purpose-driven life*

- *Uzziah's anointing for technological advancement*

- *The disciples' anointing for learning*

- *Jabez's anointing for territorial and intellectual growth*

- *Eve's anointing for fruitfulness and dominion*

Lord, cause these apostolic and prophetic anointings to converge, explode, and be manifested in my life with accuracy, authenticity, clarity, and elegance. In Jesus's name, amen.[5]

❧ LET IT BE to ME . . .

You've already started the closing exercise for this chapter by making faith-filled declarations to God according to His Word about the anointing upon your life. *Now I ask you again: What has God specifically anointed you to do as you answer the call to go?* Are you facing a test that looks much bigger than you could possibly handle? Let's build on the exercise you did at the end of chapter 1.

Take a few moments and prayerfully consider the following questions: Are you crystal clear about what God is calling you to do? Is there a miraculous flow of the anointing as you follow Him? Are you ready to believe God for the impossible and go to the next level of your calling? I challenge you to trust God and see yourself as the mighty warrior He has called you to be. Then, by the power of the Holy Spirit, do everything God requires you to do and declare the victory…because *you are anointed for this!*

four

THE ANOINTING *of* TRUE WORSHIP

The time is coming—it has, in fact, come—when what you're called will not matter and where you go to worship will not matter. It's who you are and the way you live that count before God. Your worship must engage your spirit in the pursuit of truth. That's the kind of people the Father is out looking for: those who are simply and honestly themselves before him in worship. God is sheer being itself—Spirit. Those who worship him must do it out of their very being, their spirits, their true selves, adoration.

—JOHN 4:23–24, THE MESSAGE

S O HOW DO we stay in the atmosphere of the anointing? How do we keep our hearts postured toward God, prepared to do what He calls us to do? Romans 12:1 comes back to mind, "Take your everyday, ordinary life—your sleeping, eating, going-to-work, and walking-around life—and place it before God as an offering" (THE MESSAGE).

I may write something right here that surprises you. People all over the world know me for my music: the songs, lyrics, and anointing that flow through me when I minister, and I cherish this! But music is not my passion. Worship is my passion! Worship is *who I am* and *what I do*. In fact, I believe my music is just an overflow of my worship. I can't imagine my life without the ability and privilege to magnify and glorify God.

This is just one of the reasons why I feel so blessed to have been born in this nation that we call the United States of America. Our constitution allows the freedom to worship as has been emphatically stated by the Founding Fathers of this nation. The US Constitution states in the First Amendment: "Congress shall make no law respecting an establishment of religion, or prohibiting the free exercise thereof."[1]

This freedom allows not only me but also everyone else who is either born in America or who emigrates here from another country the right to assemble and worship whom or whatever we wish. We have the right to adopt whatever belief system we choose. That is real freedom. My heart still aches and yearns for all people of all nations to choose the one true, living God to worship. The Lord Jesus Christ is the answer to all of the ills of this world.

WE ARE CREATED TO WORSHIP GOD

I love to worship. At a very early age I was taught to give God all my worship. I saw my mom worship in all sorts of scenarios; her life was consumed with two things: children and worship. Being the baby of twelve, I knew the cost of her oil. Worship was everything to her. She knew that worshipping God would get her through whatever came her way. My father, a very robust and hardworking farmer, would get up every morning around four or five o'clock, before his day got started, in order to spend time with God in prayer and worship. I saw my siblings spend regular time with God, especially my sisters. Nothing was more important in our home when we were growing up than serving and worshipping God.

Coming from that culture of prayer, praise, and worship, it was natural for me, as the youngest of twelve siblings, to be greatly influenced by a lifestyle of devotion to God. He was all that we had and all that we needed. Now, as a mother of two teenagers, it is imperative for my husband and me to instill in our girls the same importance of worshipping God. Jamie and I do this on a regular basis, because we want them to understand that prayer, praise, and worship make the difference in whether or not they will win the battles of life or live in defeat.

When I wake up in the morning, right before I get out of the bed, I try to pause and thank God for the incredible opportunity to wake up…and so I worship. David said, "From the rising of the sun unto the going down of the same the LORD's name is to be praised" (Ps. 113:3, KJV). David knew the importance of keeping praise and worship on his lips. All the things he faced gave him the ability to learn that victory came only by surrendering to a lifetime of worship.

When young David wrote songs and tended to his father's sheep, he worshipped. (See Psalms 8; 19.) When he had to face the lion and the bear to protect the sheep, I can imagine David lifting his eyes to heaven and asking God for help, and then worshipping after each episode. When he was being chased by Saul, David found comfort in worshipping God Almighty and writing psalms to Him. (See Psalms 57; 59.) Many years later when he and Bathsheba lost their first son, he worshipped (2 Sam. 12:15–20). When David failed God miserably, he worshipped. (See Psalm 51.) Time after time, no matter what he was facing, David always came back to the altar of prayer and worship.

Like David, we too must learn to worship and "bless the LORD at all times" (Ps. 34:1.) His praise should *continually* fill our mouths! When I wake up in the morning and think of the alternative to waking up, I love to worship God. So when I open my eyes and am still breathing, I worship. When it comes to my remembrance that my feet are still working, my arms are still working, and my legs are still walking, I worship. When I recall that I can still talk and yawn and see the beautiful sunshine outside, I worship the Lord.

I thank God that I live in a nice, warm house during the cold months and a cool house during the hot months. When I go downstairs and get to choose what I am going to eat for breakfast, I keep worshipping Him. When I get into a bathtub with hot water, I worship. I thank God that I have a *bathroom* because I used to have a *path* (i.e., an outside toilet), and I worship.

When I hug my husband and whisper, "Good morning," I worship in my heart because I remember that when I was in my thirties, I didn't even have a boyfriend to take me out on dates, much less a husband. So I thank the Lord every day for this godly Boaz whom He has sent into my life…and I worship Him. Every time the wheels of an airplane hit the runway safely, I worship God. When we come back from long trips on planes, trains, and automobiles all over the world, join ourselves back together as a family, and everyone is safe and sound, I worship.

I will bless the Lord at all times, and His praise will continually be in my mouth! When I hear those now "big feet" (instead of those little, tiny feet) come trampling down the stairs, I worship God, because I remember a time when the doctor said I couldn't have children. And now, look at God! We have *two* children! So I worship!

Have you ever thought about what Jesus said the ramifications are if we don't worship? When the Pharisees told Jesus to rebuke His disciples for lifting praises to God, He answered, "I tell you that if these should keep silent, the stones would immediately cry out" (Luke 19:40).

Everything God made in the beginning was created to worship: the trees reaching to the sky; the wind and waves churning; the moon when it shines; the sun when it beats down on our brows; the flowers that release beautiful fragrances; the gigantic sharks in the ocean; the dolphins as they sing, squeal, or dance across the water—everything that God created gives worship to Him. But nothing moves Him like our worship. That's why David could declare in Psalm 150:6, "Let everything that has breath praise the LORD. Praise the LORD!"

WORSHIP—OUR REASONABLE SACRIFICE

When we place the moments of our lives before God as a continual offering, we are giving Him the true worship He desires. Sometimes we have to worship the Lord by giving Him a "sacrifice of praise" (Heb. 13:15). At some point in our Christian walk we all have to count the cost of living out our faith.

I will never forget as long as I live witnessing a sacrifice of praise. I was a part of Mike and Deann Barber's "Weekend of Excitement," which hosted about eight hundred women and seven hundred men in the same weekend. These men and women were in maximum security prisons and had found Jesus during some of the most desperate times of their lives. It is during these weekends that many of them are visited in their prison cells and invited to the evening revival services. Jail and prison ministry is still one of the most exciting things that I love to do.

As I was sitting in the auditorium reading the Word and going over my notes, I suddenly heard a commotion coming from the prison yards. A Kirk Franklin CD was already pumping as loud as possible, and here they came, all these women, walking in a single line…and some of them were already in sync with Kirk's music. They came in bee-bopping, singing, swaying, dancing, and grooving with the music. They were obviously so glad to have the opportunity to come to service, to the "house of God," and get out of their prison cells.

It is really a sight to behold all of them in their white jumpsuits— young, old, and middle-aged; black, white, Hispanic, and Asian.

All types of women were there. The whole time I was asking the question in my mind, "Why in the world are you women here? You look so normal, so innocent, so shy and seemingly harmless." Yet there was a specific reason why each of these women was there. For a brief moment they forgot about themselves; maybe someone did something to their children, to them, or to someone they love, and in that instant they lost control and did the unthinkable! I don't know all their stories, but it sure was interesting to look across that room and see many of them coming in for a word from the Lord, a song, or maybe just a change of scenery.

As the ladies came in, they had already been instructed to go into a designated line in the row of seats, and no one was allowed to sit down until all the seats were occupied. Then they all sat down at one time together on that particular row. On and on it went like that, until the last person came in and the entire place was filled. There was one thing about the rules when they came in and sat down: once they sat down, they could not, for any reason, get up again until it was time to get in a single file and leave. If an inmate got up out of her seat, she risked the chance that she would be taken out of the room and sent to solitary confinement for breaking the rules. So coming into the auditorium, they already knew the rules and the consequences for breaking them.

One of the things that thrilled me was watching them worship. I remember watching as the praise and worship began to swell in the auditorium. Since they couldn't get up out of their seats and stand on their feet, they just moved around in their seats: bopping, clapping, moving their legs and feet and the bottom of their (hmm) seats. It's really something to see when people are so passionate about worship. They will find a way to worship God with all of their beings somehow.

The atmosphere was charged that night with the presence of God. As I got up to minister the Word, these ladies were definitely pulling on my anointing. As the Word went forth, there was one lady in particular who really got it. I mean, she got it so much that it reached the point when she counted the cost. It was as if she had made up her mind, "This is my Word. I'm not going to stay in my seat any longer; I *have* to praise Him!" All of a sudden she got up out of her chair and began to dance before the Lord, shouting, hollering, and praising God with all that she had within her.

At that very minute two security guards came, both kind of up in age. I honestly don't think either of them had ever been around someone having a "Holy Ghost fit" before, so, first of all, they were trying to catch this lady, get their hands on her, and get her subdued. (It was actually quite hilarious when I think about it now, but then it was *glorious* and a little unsettling!) We managed to make sure that none of the other prisoners got up out of their seats (even with all the praise going on), but as they were dragging her out, she was still bucking and shouting, kicking and crying, and laughing and worshipping, all at the same time. I can't tell you what happened after that. All I know is *that woman got a word from the Lord*, she had to *move* with that Word, and she gave God a sacrifice of praise.

When I look back on that incident, I think about some of the churches where I have ministered. It sometimes feels like you are trying to pull teeth to get someone to lift their hands, much less stand on their feet and give God a shout of praise. I wonder what it would be like for us if that kind of restraint was ever put on our churches.

How much would the believers in the Chinese house churches love it if they could clap their hands as loud as they wanted, sing as loud as they wanted, talk about God as loud as they wanted, and (how about this one) meet together as often as they wanted, as long as they wanted? Consider the 10/40 window—a part of the world that has the most people on the planet yet where the people are the least evangelized and Christians are the most persecuted.

Sometimes God is going to test you and see if you are willing to move when He moves. At times He'll test your resolve in what He has for you, because you can't dictate to the Holy Spirit how He is going to deliver you and bring you through a certain situation. You just have to trust Him and walk in obedience. And when you do, God will honor your act of worship.

Setting an Atmosphere of Worship

Recently during a trip to Washington DC to have some writing time and meet a few friends, we decided to do a little sightseeing. One of the first places we visited was Mount Vernon, the home of America's first president, George Washington. This was not the first time that I had visited Mount Vernon, but it was the first time for some of our friends. I had seen the beautiful, picturesque family plantation located near Alexandria, Virginia. The plantation was built in the 1700s in a "neoclassical Georgian architectural style, and the estate is located on the banks of the Potomac River" across from Prince George County, Maryland.[2]

There was an absolutely amazing view from every corner in the house. I was stunned by every room. Since we were there in December, we had a great surprise; that is the month when they actually open up the third floor for visitors to see the private family floor where the Washingtons lived at one time. Again, these sights are only seen once a year, so we felt especially privileged to be able to view this part of Mount Vernon.

As we made our way through each room in the mansion, we were greeted by a historic interpreter. They were there to offer specific details about the "personality" of the room, so that we could actually envision it as it was used over two hundred years ago. My favorite part of the mansion was the actual private floor and living space for the Washingtons. We saw the linens, the beautiful off-white quilt, the pillows, the desk, the chairs, the basin for hand-washing, and the unique fireplace. In addition, we were able to view the room that Mrs. Washington moved into when President Washington died. Everything there represented the elite lifestyle of the first president and his family during the eighteenth century. Each room told its own story out loud—in fact, very loudly.

That is the way our homes should be. Each room should speak of the anointing of God. There should be some sort of representation of the fragrance and impartation of the anointing left over in each room—your quiet place where you meet with the Lord each day to enjoy sweet fellowship; your kitchen, where you have seen God provide bread and water; your bathroom, where you have been able to wash yourself clean from the filth of this world and come out feeling fresh and renewed in the Spirit. I could go on, but I think you get where I'm going.

Creating an atmosphere for the anointing is so important in our own lives, in the lives of our family members, and in our everyday walk with the Lord. I remember as a child and later on as a teenager watching my mom leave an atmosphere for the anointing every-where she went. She was such a worshipper that if need be, she created an atmosphere for the Holy Spirit to work in. There were many times in the grocery store when people, particularly women, would come up to her and ask for prayer for their husbands, families, or bodies.

Whatever the case was, there were times she would try to find a secluded place to pray, but most often she wasn't ashamed to lift up praise and prayers to her God right where she stood. Right there she would begin to exalt the Lord and speak faith into them, declaring what the Word said about them and their lives. That's what I call true worship. She would minister to women about their marriages and families, and then with almost no hesitation she would lift her voice and begin to pray, stepping right into the atmosphere of what she knew in the spirit was the right time and place.

Sometimes we can't wait for the "perfect" atmosphere; we have to move when God says to move or when we feel an "unction" from the Holy Spirit to move (we will talk about this in a later chapter). I remember as a child watching my mom on the farm. Whether she was outside hanging clothes on the clothesline, working in the garden, or preparing meals in the kitchen for our family, when the Spirit of God touched her, she would quit whatever she was doing and move with what the Spirit was leading her to do. I saw my dad come in from the fields more than once and had to wait on lunch, simply because Mom had been with Jesus. Both of my parents were true worshippers. That's just the way it was!

Jesus responds to an atmosphere that is charged with worship, and He won't hesitate to change an atmosphere that lacks it. For example, when Jesus entered the temple as the Anointed One in Mark 11:15–17, He created a new atmosphere. (Remember, when the anointing enters darkness, it exposes and destroys that which is not anointed.) As He turned over the tables of the money changers, He was changing the atmosphere. He was creating an atmosphere of worship when He emphatically stated, "It is written, My house is the house of prayer: but ye have made it a den of thieves" (Luke 19:46, KJV) Thus Jesus changed the atmosphere in the temple from *marketing* back to *ministry*. The Word declares, "The yoke shall be destroyed because of the anointing" (Isa. 10:27, KJV).

The Power of Worship and Praise

As we have seen, praising God in song can also create an atmosphere for the anointing. Think about it. Music has been used by advertising agencies to create certain moods, which stir up a hunger for their products. Likewise movie producers use music to create special emotions in specific scenes during a film. Yes, as humans, we respond to an atmosphere.

If you want your house to be anointed, then you must change the atmosphere. Indeed, music can create an atmosphere of worship. Turn on praise music instead of watching soap operas. Pray and sing aloud in your home rather than playing video games (which, by the way, are usually filled with violence). Praise can be the "antibiotic" that purifies the atmosphere and destroys the bacteria of fear, doubt, unbelief, depression, despair, defeat, and even death. Then the purified atmosphere is conducive for the anointing to flow.

During the past few days the weather has been very muggy. The temperature has been fairly warm for winter, which has produced several mornings of heavy fog because of the high humidity and the lack of wind. However, one strong cold front can blow away the fog, drop the temperature, and clear the air and sky as nothing else can. Similarly one breath from God can clear away your "fog" and bring clear skies and pure air, which in turn can allow the anointing to flow freely again in your life.

Jack Hayford has interesting things to say about how praise can change the atmosphere. In his book *Prayer Is Invading the Impossible* he states: "Praise is not intended to compliment God. Some people have confessed quite candidly…that praise seems like an effort to curry God's favor by smoothing or massaging His heavenly ego.… [But praise] is an instrument of violence. Praise upsets the climate which furthers the growth of much of life's suffering, confusion, turmoil, and strife. Praise destroys the atmosphere in which sickness, defeat, discouragement, and futility flourish. Praise beats out hell's brush fires. Praise breathes heaven's life into the vacuum death produces on earth."[3]

I love for my in-laws (or as I say, my *in-loves* because I love them so dearly) to come and visit our home as much as possible. Whenever my mother-in-love steps in, she always says the same thing: "I love coming to your house. There is such a peace here and such a sweet spirit of God that is here." I adore hearing that because I want Him (the Holy Spirit) to always be our special guest in our house and never, ever leave.

People often ask me, especially when I'm on the road, "What is it about my house?" Their kids are always fighting, the parents speak down to each other, and the family is endlessly squabbling over something. I immediately ask what kind of atmosphere is created and sustained in their homes. Prayer, praise, and thanksgiving can change a negative atmosphere into a positive one that is immediately alive with God's Spirit and anointing.

If you want the Holy Spirit to feel at home in your house, you have to create an atmosphere that is conducive to Him. He will not stay where He doesn't feel comfortable. So if you want Him to be in your home constantly, play praise music or even sing it yourself. Speak peaceably to your spouse, your kids…even to yourself. Proclaim blessings over your family as they walk through the door and see for yourself how the anointing can rush in. You are anointed for worship. Set the tone for the anointing in your home.

Our daughters' rooms are somewhat connected to each other. One day I went into each of their rooms to pray for them after they had gone to school. When I lay down in Kaylee's bed, I felt the anointing very strongly. When I mentioned this to her later, she related to me what had happened the night before. She told me, "Mom, after we had prayer time together and said good night, I had an intimate time in the Word and in prayer and worship that lasted for a couple of hours." I told her what had happened to me after she left for school, and before the day was over not only had she experienced it again, but also her sister and some friends who came over found themselves on the floor weeping before the Lord, enjoying the presence of God. That atmosphere was still lingering the next day and even into the night. That is powerful!

OUR LIFESTYLE OF WORSHIP

Our prayers and our praise are powerfully effective because they reflect a lifestyle of worship. I love to see it this way:

- *Worship* is related to *who He is*, knowing that He is Lord.

- *Praise* is related to *what He is*, knowing that He is *worthy*.

- *Prayer* is related to *what He can do*, knowing that He is both *willing* and *able* to do "exceedingly abundantly above all that we ask or think, *according to the power* [anointing, *dunamis*[4]] that works in us" (Eph. 3:20, emphasis added).

When worship is *who we are* and *what we do*, when it is our life-style, we have the ability to change the atmosphere around us and be an influence for good in any situation. Why? God's dynamic power, His anointing, goes to work in ways we could never imagine.

This reminds me of Mark 16:15–18. Jesus said, "Go into all the world and preach the gospel to every creature.... And these signs will follow those who believe: In My name they will cast out demons; they will speak with new tongues; they will take up serpents; and if they drink anything deadly, it will by no means hurt them; they will lay hands on the sick, and they will recover."

In other words, by the power of the Holy Spirit we can take charge of the atmosphere around us, injecting a dynamic, positive anointing into negative situations. We can bring light into darkness, declare healing to displace sickness, declare deliverance to set captives free, and yes, even make dead things come alive again.

Remember, if we're not *saying it* (the Word and will of God), then we won't *see it* (His will and purposes come to pass). Declaring the Word is an act of obedience and worship. When our heart is bathed in worship, we can speak peace, speak life, and see dynamic change. Proverbs 25:11 says, "A word fitly spoken is like apples of gold in settings of silver." Words spoken by the power of the anointing produce fruit that will last for eternity.

This brings me back to David, who surrendered to a lifetime of worship. He blessed the Lord at all times. Whether his circumstances were good or bad, David maintained a posture of worshipping God in his heart. This resulted in a life that consistently showed forth the glory of God. And even when David fell short of God's glory, he quickly returned to God again and again, walking out his life as "a man after His own heart" (1 Sam. 13:14).

When I think of young David's victory over Goliath, I remember his declaration in Psalm 144:1: "Praise the Lord, who is my rock. He trains my hands for war and gives my fingers skill for battle" (NLT). This is such a testimony to God! He used David's very hands and fingers to win this decisive battle for the entire nation of Israel. When God moved upon David by the power of the anointing, he picked up five little stones…and by throwing just one of them, he overthrew a giant who had been setting an atmosphere to defeat Israel by declaring, "I defy the armies of Israel this day" (1 Sam. 17:10).

But when David first arrived at the battle scene and heard Goliath's confession with a heart that continually worshipped God, the first thing he said was, "What shall be done for the man who kills this Philistine and takes away the reproach from Israel? For who is this uncircumcised Philistine, that he should defy the armies of the living God?" (v. 26). David changed the atmosphere by declaring the victory for Israel and speaking death to the enemy. And then he walked it out. When Goliath went down, David immediately chopped off his head. That enemy would never rise again.

Keep this picture in your mind, because that's what we do when we place our everyday lives—our sleeping, eating, going-to-work, and walking-around life—before God as an offering. Every time we worship God, whether it's in word, deed, or song, we chop off the devil's head. And when we clap our hands, stomp our feet, play an instrument, open our mouths and sing praises to God, nurse someone back to health, lead and administrate in the marketplace, or simply give someone a cup of cold water in His name, we are using our gifts to bring an all-out assault against the evil one.

What I have learned is that *when you are anointed, the atmosphere of your heart qualifies you to be used by God.* Philippians 2:13 declares, "For God is working in you, giving you the desire and the power to do what pleases him" (NLT). God is constantly doing something in our lives. Sometimes we like it; sometimes we don't. Sometimes it's good; sometimes it's epic! But if we are ever going to be used by God, sometimes God Himself creates the atmosphere for growth, dependence, strength, and anointing. I don't know about you, but this makes me want to stop right now and worship God with all that is within me.

Father God is seeking true worshippers, and He responds to our worship. Jesus made a promise to all who walk out their lives as *people after God's own heart.* He declared:

> The person who has My commands and keeps them is the one who [really] loves Me; and whoever [really] loves Me will be loved by My Father, and I [too] will love him and will show (reveal, manifest) Myself to him. [I will let Myself be clearly seen by him and make Myself real to him.]
> —JOHN 14:21, AMP

The next time you need to change the atmosphere, remember that God has created you to worship Him. True worship is part of your spiritual DNA. You can rise up in your everyday life, loving God in everything you do, and set an atmosphere for the anointing to thrive.

∞ LET IT BE to ME . . .

Part of walking with God day to day, prepared to obey Him as He leads you into purpose, is living a life of true worship. Worship sets an atmosphere that allows you to walk in the anointing and authority of God over the enemy. When you worship God and declare His Word, you are posturing yourself to do "greater works" that will last for eternity.

I trust you are convinced that you can set the atmosphere wherever you go, starting in your own heart and home. So let me ask you: How fruitful have you been in setting an atmosphere for the anointing: (1) In your heart?, (2) In your home?, (3) In your work and ministry?, and (4) Wherever you go?

Considering this chapter, what do you need to change in order to walk consistently in the anointing of true worship? If you haven't been keeping a journal, now is the time to start, because a heart of love and worship to God is foundational to releasing His anointing. Now, go to God, journal your thoughts, and worship Him for helping you do all that is required…because He gives you the desire and power to do what pleases Him. I'll say it again: *you are anointed for this!*

five

THE ANOINTED PRAY-ER

I bow before your holy Temple as I worship. I praise your name for your unfailing love and faithfulness; for your promises are backed by all the honor of your name. As soon as I pray, you answer me; you encourage me by giving me strength.

—PSALM 138:2–3, NLT

W E, AS THE body of Christ, are called to pray: both corporately and individually. As we obey this calling and demonstrate true worship to God through our prayers, He is ready, willing, and able to make Himself real to us. Oswald Chambers wrote: "The purpose of prayer is that we get ahold of God, not of the answer."[1] Amen! Because 2 Corinthians 1:20 says, "For all the promises of God *in Him* are Yes, and *in Him* Amen, to the glory of God through us" (emphasis added).

With this in mind Jesus said: "And when you pray..." (Matt. 6:5), "Moreover, when you fast..." (v. 16), and "When you give..." (v. 2, NLT). These three "when" statements imply that God expects us to do these things, so they are foundational in our walk with Him. I believe that as we demonstrate true worship and live out our Christian walk in purity and complete devotion to the Lord, we can put a demand on our prayers. We can expect God to answer when we pray anointed prayers to Him in faith.

You may have heard of the "fight or flight syndrome," a medical condition that describes the body's natural response to stress and danger. During times of stress in our lives, especially when we are faced with split-second decisions, we have to determine if we are going to stand and fight or run with everything in us. Unfortunately that is where a lot of Christians find themselves many times, and more often than not, there is more *flight* than *fight*. Now is the time we have to stand our ground and be determined that we will not run in the face of adversity. No! We will stand, flat-footed and firm, on the fact that our God, Jehovah, is a faithful Father who hears and answers prayer.

Prayer is one of the most powerful weapons we can use to fight against our enemy. Yet, so many Christians fail to use this highly effective weapon. James 5:16 says, "The effective, fervent prayer of a righteous man avails much." Maybe the devil has been telling you that you're not righteous enough. Well, let me assure you, if the blood of Jesus has been applied to your life, then God sees you as *justified*; i.e., "just as if" you never sinned.[2] Remember, He throws our sins into the sea of forgetfulness, never to be brought against us anymore. Psalm 103:12 says, "As far as the east is from the west, so far has He removed our transgressions from us." Remember, my friend, the blood is enough!

So, in this pursuit of knowing we are anointed for this, we need to establish that *the devil is an unmitigated, unqualified, and absolutely relentless liar!* You are *everything* that God says you are, and you are *nothing* that the devil says you are. By faith in the Lord Jesus Christ and His finished work, you can boldly approach God's throne of grace in prayer, knowing you'll find mercy and grace to help you, and anyone you might be praying for, in times of need (Heb. 4:16). You are anointed for this!

GOD HEARS THE PRAYER OF FAITH

It is worth mentioning again that our family, both at home and in church, reminds one another often about *seeing it* and *saying it*. Friend, if we're not "seeing it," it's probably because we're not "saying it." We must continually remind ourselves and our children what the Word says about us. That keeps faith alive. In Deuteronomy 6:7 God told the children of Israel, "Repeat them again and again to your children. Talk about them when you are at home and when are on the road, when you are going to bed and when you are getting up" (NLT).

Even before we remind each other, by faith we should remind God of what He has *said* in His Word by *saying* it to Him in prayer. This is declaring our faith, and God hears the prayer of faith! Robert Morgan writes that the power of the Word is:

> …a force to be reckoned with, containing intrinsic power, high enough to give insight, deep enough to give us peace, wide enough to mold our personalities, and strong enough to bear us through horrendous days.[3]

Can I get an amen? As I write this chapter, I can hardly believe what I am about to share with you about some very special people in my life—my daughters. Through the years as I have written books and recorded music, I have had opportunities to dedicate these very special moments not only to my daughters but also to my wonderful husband. Now, once again, I find myself writing about these strong young women of God, who were once two little people in my life. I am witnessing faith come into sight in their lives…praise God! Kaylee and Erica are two of the most anointed young women I know. Like me, they still have a long way to go yet (smiles), but still, they are deeply in love with Jesus.

I love to hear them sing, play their instruments, harmonize with each other, preach, and teach, but I really love to hear them pray.

They are some of the most powerful prayer warriors I have ever heard. Of course, they have been doing it for quite a while. My thirteen-year-old is one of the most strategic prayer warriors I have seen, especially for someone attending middle school. Kaylee, my sixteen-year-old, has been praying and prophesying since she was just a little thing. I still remember a time when she challenged us as a little girl.

She must have been around four years old, and her sister was about a year old. I was very sick with bronchitis. I had been to the doctor and was on medication; it was a trying time for my husband because he was taking care of me and the two girls. Somehow all of us ended up on our bed one night, so Jamie told the girls, "Come on, girls…let's pray for Mom, and then we have to get ready to go to bed." So after a long day of taking care of three girls, he began to pray. Consequently he was exhausted. Let's just say his prayer that night was a little short of being "fervent."

As Jamie was praying a very somber and "hurry-up-so-I-can-get-little-people-in-bed-and-me-too" kind of prayer, Kaylee suddenly blurted out, "Stop! Wait a minute, Daddy. You're not praying right. We've got to get up and start walking and praying *real loud and hard* for Mommy to be healed." She got up off the bed and began to lead the prayer. Off she went, with her daddy following her lead. I tell you, that little baby prayed hard, which left nothing else for her daddy to do except follow suit. Baby Erica was staring at all of us with her bottle in her mouth looking like, "These people have lost their minds."

Well, you know what happened? The Spirit of the Lord hit me! I began to weep, her daddy was weeping, and I got up off the bed and began to praise God. He touched me and healed me that night, and the next morning I got up refreshed and delivered. *If God said it, it will happen,* and the vehicle we use to get His attention and get to the place we desire is faith and prayer. Watch out, because sometimes He will use those "babes... [to] silence the enemy and the avenger" (Ps. 8:2). Praise God!

Not too long ago we were asked to go to Barranquilla, Colombia, to attend a very powerful ladies conference. We were having services in a beautiful ballroom filled with more than twenty-five hundred women who were attending to seek the face of God and believe for miracles. One lady in particular was enjoying her time there with some other sisters from her church when she got a phone call from her son that her husband was very ill and that she needed to come home to attend to him. She was three hours from home. But before she left, I was finishing up my message about Lazarus and how Jesus waited until the fourth day to show up, when nothing could be done about his death.

The Jews believed that the spirit of a man would hover over a body for three days, and then by some sort of miracle, maybe, just maybe, he could be raised from the dead—but not after the fourth day. Then it was utterly impossible.[4] This makes it more than obvious why Jesus waited until the fourth day to go to Bethany. (See John 11:1–44, esp. vv. 1–17.) Remember, with men many things are impossible, but with God *all* things are possible!

So I was preaching this message about Lazarus declaring, "It is the fourth day, and everything that is dead has to get up, wake up, and come alive in your lives." The power of God was very strong as the Word was going forth; I knew that people were receiving the rhema word of the Lord and that lives were being changed forever. When the woman got the phone call, she left immediately and started her journey home. On the way home she began to feel an intense urge to begin praying very aggressively in the Spirit for her husband. When she got home, she was greeted by her son, who informed her that his father had died three hours ago.

This lady never lost her faith. James 1:6–8 says, "But when you pray, you must believe and not doubt at all. Whoever doubts is like a wave in the sea that is driven and blown about by the wind. If you are like that, unable to make up your mind and undecided in all you do, you must not think that you will receive anything from the Lord" (GNT). She stood strong and did not believe or receive this report.

She went in the room, and sure enough, her husband was dead...so she began to worship. Then the anointing came forcibly into the room and she began to speak to his body, commanding him to come back to life. She did this on and on, and then after a while he started to get warm; then all of a sudden he began to breathe. That man literally came back to life. Praise God, He answers prayer! Bold prayer! Violent prayer! Confident prayer!

There is an anointing that can literally transform your prayer life so you will see the supernatural take place right before your eyes. Prayer is necessary. Prayer is powerful. Prayer is effective. Mary Alessi, a friend of mine, an anointed fellow songwriter and recording artist and copastor of Metro Life Church in Miami, Florida, has this to say about the anointing:

> Passionate, powerful, and dynamic are just few words to describe "the anointing." When you are anointed, you are dramatically inspired to never stop seeking God for more of Him. You speak with a boldness that is unparalleled and from a place of revelation and understanding of real, godly authority. For those desiring that, I think it pretty much covers every believer![5]

I have to agree again with the words of Oswald Chambers: "The purpose of prayer is that we get ahold of God, not of the answer." There have been plenty of times when I was seeking answers from God, but when it was all said and done, I had received such an experience with God and such a depth with Him that I was thankful for the journey. It is during those times that you really get anointed to pray. When you don't know what an outcome is going to be, you pray as if your life depends on it, because quite frankly, your life does depend on it. During those times no demon or devil in hell can take that experience away from you. And you will find that you have gained a history with God—not your mama's God or your daddy's God but *your* God!

GOD WANTS TO HEAR FROM YOU

Remember, when Jesus said "And when you pray…" in Matthew 6:5, He implied that God absolutely expects you to communicate with Him. Prayer is necessary and should be done *on purpose,* intentionally and regularly, every day. You will find that when you are praying in the anointing, distractions come less, but more than anything you discover that you are not bothered by distractions.

When you are anointed to pray, you're not listening to the eloquence of your words. Your heart is so tuned into God and the Holy Spirit that mere words are just that: words. You find yourself pouring out your very soul to Him, and at the same time you know you are touching heaven. This is the meaning of one of the forms of prayer in the Bible: *proseuchomai,* "to supplicate, worship," or in other words, "to pour out."[6] In essence, Jesus asked His disciples in the garden three times if they could not "pour themselves out" for Him for one hour. (See Matthew 26:41–42, 44.)

Also, this is the kind of prayer in James 5:17. God wants to hear heartfelt, hot, and weighty prayers that are prayed in faith. You see, it is our faith that moves Him. The Bible says, "But without faith it is impossible to please Him, for he who comes to God must believe that He is, and that He is a rewarder of those who diligently seek Him" (Heb. 11:6).

Prayer is powerful. I don't care who you are or where you came from; you can be assured of this: *God hears and answers prayer.* The Word declares, "Now this is the confidence that we have in

Him, that if we ask anything according to His will, He hears us. And if we know that He hears us, whatever we ask, we know that we have the petitions that we have asked of Him" (1 John 5:14–15). OK, that that settles it! I'll say it again: *God hears the prayer that is prayed in faith.*

In his book *Prayer Is Invading the Impossible*, Jack Hayford says: "The impossible faces us all. It storms, fumes, looms before us, stalks our days, presses upon our minds, bends our plans, stands formidably across our future, pierces our present, reaches out from the past. But there is a way to face impossibility. *Invade it!* Not with a glib speech of high hopes. Not in anger. Not with resignation. Not through stoical self-control. But with violence. And prayer provides the vehicle for this kind of violence."[7]

That is exactly what God did with the children of Israel. The Bible records the brutality of what they had to endure under a new pharaoh who arose over Egypt, "who knew nothing about Joseph or what he had done" (Exod. 1:8, NLT). So as the story goes, Pharaoh's daughter found baby Moses in the bushes, and she took him as her son and raised him in the palace. But things went south very quickly, because Moses began to get very inquisitive about his life and found out that he was indeed an Israelite and that he was adopted by the king's daughter. He went out one day and saw an Egyptian soldier mistreating his fellow Israelite, and he killed him. Word got back to the king about this crime, so Moses fled in terror from the wrath of Pharaoh. (See Exodus 1:8–2:15.)

Meantime the children of Israel did not stop praying and asking God for deliverance. The Bible records their desperate cry:

> Years passed, and the king of Egypt died. But the Israelites continued to groan under their burden of slavery. They cried out for help, *and their cry rose up to God.* God heard their groaning, and he *remembered* his covenant promise

to Abraham, Isaac, and Jacob. He looked down upon the people of Israel and knew *it was time to act.*
—EXODUS 2:23–25, NLT, EMPHASIS ADDED

YOU CAN EXPRESS YOURSELF FREELY IN PRAYER

Now let's look at prayer more closely. There are several different words used in the Bible that translate from Greek to English as the word *prayer.* So different expressions of prayer are already in your spirit. As you pray to God in faith, they begin to flow freely from your inner man.

- *Euchomai* is the simplest form of prayer. It is translated as, "to wish; by implication, to pray to God."[8]
This is used in 3 John 2: "Beloved, I wish [pray] above
all things that thou mayest prosper and be in health,
even as thy soul prospereth" (KJV).

- *Proseuchomai* is a burden resulting in "pouring out"
in prayer. As stated earlier, this is the kind of prayer
that Jesus prayed in the Garden of Gethsemane. This
word can also describe the prayers that are referred
to in Revelation 5:8 as the "golden vials full of odours
[bowls of incense], which are the prayers of the saints"
in Revelation 5:8 (KJV).

- *Dorea,* according to Pastor Desmond T. Evans, is the
Greek word *gift,* meaning a "creative prayer" from
praying in the Spirit. This kind of prayer is mentioned in Romans 8:26, "Likewise the Spirit also hel-
peth our infirmities: for we know not what we should
pray for as we ought: but the Spirit itself maketh
intercession for us with groanings which cannot be
uttered" (KJV). Pastor Jack Hayford describes this
kind of prayer as "private," while the gift of tongues

is a "public" gift.[9] (See Acts 2:38; 1 Corinthians 14:15; Ephesians 6:18.)

- *Entugchano* is intercession, which is pleading the cause of someone else.[10] Hebrews 7:25 says that Jesus "ever liveth to make intercession" for us (KJV). The original language, according to Pastor Evans, says, "We call forth those things which were foreordained in the heavens that they would come to pass into the now in our human experience."[11]

Now, do you remember James 5:16, "The effective, fervent prayer of a righteous man avails much"? That word for "prayer" is *deesis*, whose root can mean "contracting with God."[12] The words *effective, fervent* come from the Greek word *energeo*, which means, "to be active, efficient"[13] and from which we get the word *energy*. In other words, our prayers are alive!

Let me give you an example of this word *energeo*. Some friends were sailing around the tip of Florida, dragging their fishing poles and bait along the ocean. They caught a mess of fish, cleaned and cut them, and then immediately cooked them—right on board. One of the guys said the fish were so fresh they were still quivering when they put them into the frying pan. That, my friend, is a picture of *energeo*. Think of your prayers as being that fresh, active, and alive in the Spirit, and they will avail much!

I am reminded of a testimony that was told by a missionary friend of mine. He was in a village in South America when revival broke out there and went on for several weeks. There was a couple in the church who were actively involved in ushering and preparing the sanctuary, so they left home early one day to arrive at church and get their duties done, leaving the kids to walk to the church later after their chores. As you know, oftentimes kids in certain parts of the world are expected to grow up faster than kids in other parts of the world.

Later on, their children (a little girl around eight or nine years old with her little brother, who was around five or six years old) were on their way to the church service. As they were going through a certain part of the jungle, all of a sudden a python snake dropped down from a tree and began to wrap itself around the little girl's body. It was very close to choking her to death while her little brother looked on in terror. As the snake was getting ready to make its last squeeze on her neck and attempting to open its mouth over her head, the little girl managed to get one word out to her little brother… "Pray!"

He barely got the words out, "In the name of Jesus…," when suddenly the snake immediately loosened its grip from his sister and writhed away. They took off running, escaping the "death squeeze" of that snake. As the kids told their testimony that night in the meeting, the little girl still had teeth marks on her head from the snake. I tell you that God hears and answers prayer—from children or adults, in America or around the world. Wherever you may be, you need to be assured that prayer is powerful and effective!

YOU CAN PRAY ALL THE WAY THROUGH TO VICTORY

Yes, no matter what the enemy tries to tell us, our prayers are effective. It really does matter, however, how we pray through until we get an answer from God. As I have already said, we must pray in faith, coming to God's throne of grace confidently and boldly, knowing we will find help there. We must pray in the authority of the name of Jesus, and sometimes we must pray violently. "What does that mean?", you might ask. I believe, as the Lord Himself said, "And from the days of John the Baptist until now the kingdom of heaven suffers violence, and the violent take it by force" (Matt. 11:12).

As one scholar puts it, "Though the Greek here is somewhat difficult to translate, the idea in this verse is that the kingdom of heaven, which Jesus set up as a powerful movement or reign among men (suffers violence), requires of them an equally strong and radical reaction. The violent then who take it by force are people of keen enthusiasm and commitment who are willing to respond to and propagate with radical abandonment the message and dynamic of God's reign."[14] *That's us!* Radical people of God. The Word says, "The people who know their God shall be strong, and carry out great exploits" (Dan. 11:32).

Jesus also said in Luke 16:16, "The law and the prophets were until John. Since that time the kingdom of God has been *preached*, and everyone is *pressing* into it" (emphasis added).

Jesus declared that the advancement of the kingdom of God is the result of two things: *preaching* and *pressing in*. That set the atmosphere for heartfelt worship and prayer. He let us know the gospel of the kingdom must be proclaimed with spiritual passion. So in every generation believers have to determine whether they will respond to this truth with sensible minds and sensitive hearts.

> To overlook [what Jesus said] will bring a passivity that limits the ministry of God's kingdom to extending the terms of truth and love—that is, teaching or educating and engaging in acts of kindness. Without question, we must do these things. However, apart from 1) an impassioned pursuit of prayer, 2) confrontation with the demonic, 3) expectation of the miraculous, and 4) a burning heart for evangelism, the kingdom of God makes little penetration in the world.... "Pressing in" is accomplished first in prayer warfare, coupled with a will to surrender one's life and self-interests, in order to gain God's kingdom goals.[15]

When you pray aggressively, authoritatively, and are anointed, something has to change—and *it will change*. The effective, fervent prayer of the righteous avails much! James 5:17–18 says, "Elias [Elijah] was a man subject to like passions as we are, and he prayed earnestly that it might not rain: and it rained not on the earth by the space of three years and six months. And he prayed again, and the heaven gave rain, and the earth brought forth her fruit" (KJV).

Did you catch the first part of that verse that said Elijah was a man of "like passions"? That means he was just like you and me. Don't sell yourself short! Let me remind you again of what Jesus said in John 14:12, "He who believes in Me, the works that I do he will do also; and greater works than these he will do, because I go to My Father." You have the "greater works" anointing inside of you.

You have been brought into the kingdom for such a time as this! Like Elijah, you can rise up in prayer and true worship and literally change the atmosphere for the glory of God! You are built to press in and *take the kingdom by force.*

It's Time to PUSH!

You are anointed to worship God with all that is in you. You are built to abide in His Word and in His presence until dynamic change comes. Read Psalm 1:1–3 with me. It starts and finishes with a blessing:

> Blessed is the man who walks not in the counsel of the ungodly, nor stands in the path of sinners, nor sits in the seat of the scornful; but his *delight* is in the law of the LORD, and in His law he *meditates* day and night. He shall be like a tree planted by the rivers of water [*the anointing!*], that brings forth its fruit in its season, whose leaf also shall not wither; and whatever he does shall prosper.
>
> —EMPHASIS ADDED

Jack Hayford writes, "If the child of God can 'pray without ceasing' (1 Thess. 5:17), and 'thank God without ceasing' (1 Thess. 2:13), then it is also possible, in the anointing of God, to *meditate day and night* on God's truth. This suggests a constant state of communion and fellowship with God" (emphasis added).[16]

At our church in Cleveland, Tennessee, we do what we call PUSH nights. "What are PUSH nights?", you might ask. These are events where we pray all night long, from 10:00 p.m. until 6:00 a.m. They are "**P**ray **U**ntil **S**omething **H**appens" nights. Sometimes you have to pray and meditate and pray some more, and then sing praise and worship and pray some more, until "something"—*God's thing*—happens.

There were times in Jesus's life when He prayed all night long. Sometimes that is what we have to do. We have to pray, either until something happens in the situation or (usually) until something happens to us. These nights of prayer are one of the most powerful things we do as a church.

Let's look at the word *meditate*. When I meditate, it means that I study and think about the Bible regularly, that I *delight* in the Scriptures. As you meditate in the Word of God, it teaches you who God is and guides you in the decisions of life. I urge you to delight in and seek time with God. The more you know Him, the more you will love to behold His matchless beauty.

The word *meditate* comes from the Hebrew word *hagah* (pronounced haw-gaw'), which means "to murmur (in pleasure or anger); by implication to ponder, imagine, meditate."[17] Sometimes during meditation one makes a quiet sound, such as sighing; to meditate or contemplate something as one repeats the words. "In Hebrew thought to meditate upon the Scriptures is to quietly repeat them in a soft, droning sound, while utterly abandoning outside distractions. From this tradition comes a specialized type of Jewish prayer called *davening*, that is, reciting texts, praying intense prayers, or getting lost in communion with God while bowing or rocking back and forth. Evidently this dynamic form of meditation goes back to David's time,"[18] hence the term starts with the first three letters of his name.

Yes, we are called to pray, and we must PUSH as we demonstrate true worship to God through our prayers! I believe we are moving into a higher level of faith to see mountains move and revival come to our churches, pastors, families, schools, universities, and yes, in every walk of life. God has promised that if we will pray, He will hear us. Prayer is the engine for the kingdom of God. So, come on, rev up that engine. Say yes to God.

∞ LET IT BE to ME . . .

A life of true worship is a life of prayer that demands God's results. Through prayer we can set an atmosphere for the anointing to *make something happen* in the earthly realm. When we pray, as Jesus set forth, we get ahold of God. Then He freely answers us, bringing dynamic change in our own lives and in the lives of the people and situations we are praying for.

Now it's time for a little meditation, if you will: How dynamic is your life of prayer? Do you take time to abide in God's presence each day? Do you flow freely when you pray, or does communicating with God feel awkward to you? Can you lift up anointed prayers of faith to God and **P**ray **U**ntil **S**omething **H**appens? If so, I know there is a mighty anointing upon your life. If not, God wants more of you. He wants you to press in and take His kingdom by force!

I pray from this day forward you will be like a tree planted by the river of the anointing. I declare by faith that you will bring forth fruit in season and prosper in your kingdom purpose! Can I get an amen? Now, take a little time and meditate on what you have learned in this chapter. Then go to God in prayer. Make sure to write down what He tells you, because there is plenty of work for you to do! Why? *You are anointed for this!*

six

THE ANOINTING *to* PROPHESY

Worship God! For the testimony of Jesus is the spirit of prophecy.

—REVELATION 19:10

THE ANOINTING TO prophesy takes us all the way back to the beginning of the anointing, to Genesis, because that is when God first declared, "Let there be..." He prophesied during all of the six days of Creation, and by the power of the Holy Spirit the Anointed One (and, I believe, all the host of heaven) went to work. Everything came into being according to God's prophetic utterance. This is the Genesis principle. Then at the end of the sixth day, "God saw everything that He had made, and indeed it was very good" (Gen. 1:31).

Let's bring a few more things back to memory. From the beginning God determined how His supernatural anointing is released: "I believe, therefore I speak." (See 2 Corinthians 4:13.) Now, let's also remember that Jesus is the Word made flesh (John 1:1–9, 14). And the Word was, is, and always will be our *final authority*. So if you believe in Jesus, the second Adam (and I know you do), you are tapped in to the spirit of prophecy. To exercise this gift you have to do what Jesus did: learn obedience. And as I said before, this starts with *saying* what the Word says about you. *If you want to see it, you have to say it!* Oh, yes, that is good. It's *very good*.

Jack Hayford writes:

> The entire Bible is a product of the Holy Spirit, who is not only "the spirit of truth" (John 16:13), but the "spirit of prophecy" (Rev. 19:10). The verb "to prophesy" (derived from Greek preposition *pro* and verb *phemi*) means "to speak forth before." The preposition "before" in this use may mean 1) "in advance" and/or 2) "in front of." Thus, "to prophesy" is a proper term to describe the proclamation of God's Word as it forecasts events. It may also describe the declaration of God's...truth and will....So, in both respects, the Bible is prophetic: a book that reveals God's will through His Word and His works, as well as a book that reveals God's plans and predictions.[1]

A Life-Changing Prophecy

Prophecy has always been a part of my life. As far back as I can remember there has always been a man or woman of God who has prophesied the word of the Lord over me—be it my mother, sisters, pastors, aunts, and ultimately, mighty generals in God's army. He has made sure to place anointed people in my life, true worshippers, who spoke a word to me in due season.

One of the greatest prophesies I received that stands out to me more than any other was spoken over me when I was just a young girl. I was ministering and leading worship at a meeting in my home town; I was excited to be able to lead worship at a time when the charismatic and Word movement had just been birthed. This movement was spreading like wildfire in our little region, and I was happy to be a part of it in any way that I could.

Marilyn Hickey was the distinguished speaker that night. She is a woman from Denver, Colorado, who was really shaking the nations with her powerful teachings. Marilyn operated in many gifts, but what was so life changing was her ability to memorize entire chapters and even books of the Bible. What really intrigued me about this woman were the gifts of the Spirit that operated in her life so tremendously. I was excited about leading worship, but I was almost more excited to be able to sit down, see Marilyn, listen to her speak, and enjoy experiencing the gifts in operation in a way that I had never seen or known before.

I remember very distinctly that the auditorium was filled to capacity. People were worshipping God with hands lifted, waving and dancing. Then at the end of worship, in a strange and different way (in my estimation at that time), on their own accord people just took off and began singing in tongues. I had seen this happen many times in services that I had attended, but I was never leading worship when it happened. So when it actually happened to me, this was a new phenomenon, and I loved every minute of it.

There was a powerful atmosphere of the anointing. What was so funny to me was that I didn't start leading the people that way; they just took off by themselves and began to sing in the Spirit. This seemed awkward at first, but then it seemed quite natural to be able to sing a "new song" to the Lord. Nobody else sang it, knew it, or had even heard it before. Yet before all was said and done, I was singing a "new song" louder than anyone else.

After the time of praise and worship someone came to the podium to introduce Marilyn. She came to the stage and almost immediately began to delve into the Word. We were all hungry for more of the Word of God, a depth like we had never been taught before. And Marilyn, being a teacher in the public school system, had plenty of practice at being a thorough teacher. But now, with the anointing on what she was saying, it was even more dynamic.

At the end of her teaching we all began to pray…and as she prayed, all of a sudden words of knowledge began to come out of her mouth, and she would direct them to many people across the room. Then words of healing and miracles started flowing. People were getting up out of wheelchairs, and then others were just receiving prophetic words and the baptism in the Holy Spirit. As she would begin to speak, she called out different people throughout the crowd: "The lady in the red dress with the navy blue sweater on," or "The gentleman with the green shirt and the black jacket." She would call them out one by one and begin to tell them specific details of their lives in the minutest details, even down to the names of specific people. The people of God were so blessed that night, including me.

What happened next is something I could only have dreamed about. I sat there watching in sheer amazement with the rest of the people; I wasn't seeing a woman but a vessel being used by God. I was in prayer, believing and hoping that maybe, just maybe, she would pick me out of the crowd. I could hardly breathe when I heard her call out over the speaker system, "Where is the young lady who led worship tonight? God has a word for her."

All at once a gentleman came with a notebook and pen in his hand and stood next to the row where I was sitting. He said, "Would you like to stand and receive the word of the Lord?" As I stood to receive the word of the Lord, this man was writing as fast as he could so that I could have the entire word written down for me to read later. I was so hungry for more of God. Marilyn began to speak to me about the gifts I had and also about the ones that were to come. She spoke of me being in front of great crowds, people from all over the world, ministering before dignitaries, presidents, and prime ministers. It was almost too much to grasp. I kept thinking to myself, "Is she really talking about me?"

She was definitely talking about me! I can tell you, as I look back on that night in the seventies, that I can honestly say God has fulfilled and continues to fulfill that word of prophecy over my life, time and time again. The testimony of Jesus is the spirit of prophecy, and God confirms His Word. You have to believe that everything God has spoken over your life will come to pass.

BELIEVE GOD AND PROPHESY

I love the word of the Lord that came to the prophet Ezekiel. The Word says in Ezekiel 37:1–10 that God told him to perform one of the greatest miracles of the Bible. God assigned him to a valley. Matter-of-factly, God picked Ezekiel up and dropped him smack-dab in the middle of the valley. But it wasn't just any ol' ordinary valley. No! It was a valley full of bones. And not just bones; they were dry bones. And not just dry bones; the Bible says they were "very dry" bones (v. 2). Not only were they very dry bones, but they were also disjointed bones. By that I mean there was an arm over here, a leg three miles down in the valley, and a foot on the far side of the valley. That's what I call disjointed!

Then God told Ezekiel to do something miraculous. Allow me to paraphrase: "Ezekiel, I want you to raise up every one of these bones, put life back into them, and then have a revival so they will become an army." How was Ezekiel going to do this? God said, "Prophesy to these bones" (v. 4).

Now let me ask you a question. How would you like that assignment? Hear the word of the Lord—you may know what I'm talking about because that is where God has dropped you, right now as you are reading this book. Everything around you is dead, lifeless, void, and ugly. You may feel like all hope is gone, like this is your lot in life, and that this is the way it will always be. But you still have some things: you still have your voice, your hands, your feet, and your mind. Most of all, you still have the living, breathing Word of God. You can speak, decree, declare, and prophesy to all that deadness around you and command it, through the *dunamis* (dynamite) anointing of the Holy Spirit, to come back to life and *live!* Why? You are anointed to prophesy! You can also prophesy with your hands. How? Remember what David declared: "He trains my hands for war and gives my fingers skill for battle" (Ps. 144:1, NLT). Whether you *speak* the Word or *do* the Word, you are flowing in the spirit of prophecy, because you are agreeing with the testimony of Jesus, the living, breathing Word of God.

I believe like this: you can clap your way to victory, you can jump your way to victory, you can definitely shout your way to victory, and I know for a fact you can dance your way to victory. Don't believe me? Ask David! Everything that God has given us is for His purpose and His plan for our lives. He is waiting on you to use it. What is in *your* hand, Moses?

There is a little book titled *As a Man Thinketh*, written by a very obscure man most people have never heard about. But his philosophy of positive thinking, of having optimism and a spirit of "I can do," is really where the positive-thinking theory came from. At its essence this book teaches us, "Our thoughts are the most important thing about us. All that we achieve or fail to achieve is the direct result of our thinking. Our thoughts are like seeds that produce crops."[2]

In *As a Man Thinketh* author James Allen wrote: "Good thoughts and actions can never produce bad results; bad thoughts and actions can never produce good results. This is but saying that nothing can come from corn but corn, nothing from nettles but nettles. Men understand this law in the natural world, and work with it; but few understand it in the mental and moral world (though its operation there is just as simple and undeviating)."[3]

The point of the matter is that we think shapes our reality. Joyce Meyer wrote a book titled *The Battlefield of the Mind*. In it she states the mind is where the real battle is fought or won. How do we win this battle in our mind? We must continually rehearse and speak those things that God has said about us: from His Word and prophecies spoken, decreed, and declared over us, our children, our marriage, our finances, our nation, our world, or whatever it may be.

Let me say this: I love that kind of spirit. I'd rather be around a positive, upbeat kind of person any day than to be around someone who always sees the glass half empty (instead of half full), a person who always has something negative to say and is never pleasant to be around.

I think Ezekiel definitely had an "I can do" attitude. I am sure that prophesying to a huge valley of dead, dry, and disjointed bones was a mind-boggling task—but he believed God and did exactly what he was told to do. Ezekiel opened his mouth and declared the word of the Lord.

YOU ARE ANOINTED TO DECLARE HIS WORD

Now, having said that, let me say this: I believe in having the right frame of mind, absolutely! But I also believe in the Word of God, the Bible. I have to have God's truth to establish my positive outlook. Francis Schaeffer called this "true truth."[4] You can believe the facts if you want to, but as for me, *give me the truth!* God's Word is truth! Romans 3:4 declares, "Indeed, let God be true but every man a liar."

I believe the Bible is the inspired, living Word of God. It is infallible, unfailing, and untouchable in its accuracy. It speaks to us about how we should think, feel, act, speak, and live in this world that we are assigned to. As we are anointed to speak the Word of God, we will begin to appropriate the Word of God (and the anointing that comes from the Word) in our hearts, "Precept upon precept...line upon line...here a little, there a little" (Isa. 28:13), until every word is established: in our hearts and minds, on earth, in the heavens, and under the earth.

As the people of God we are anointed to change our cities, societies, nations, governments, and the world, just as God anointed and appointed Ezekiel to bring change in the nation of Israel. He has dropped us smack-dab in the middle of where He wants us to be in this world, and He wants us to make an eternal difference: prophesy to the very dry, disjointed bones, speak life, and let God use us to bring about a mighty revival in the earth.

But in order for us to declare the Word of the Lord into darkness and change the spiritual atmosphere, we have to *change our minds*! Take a little time to meditate on the following scriptures. Slow down; let them cycle through your mind and anoint your thoughts. I pray the spirit of prophecy would come upon you as you renew your mind in the Word.

> You will keep him in perfect peace whose mind is stayed on You, because he trusts in You.
>
> —ISAIAH 26:3

> For those who live according to the flesh set their minds on the things of the flesh, but those who live according to the Spirit, the things of the Spirit. For to be carnally minded is death, but to be spiritually minded is life and peace.
>
> —ROMANS 8:5–6

> Be transformed by the renewing of your mind, that you may prove what is that good and acceptable and perfect will of God.
>
> —ROMANS 12:2

> Let the Spirit renew your thoughts and attitudes. Put on your new nature, created to be like God—true, righteous and holy.
>
> —EPHESIANS 4:23–24, NLT

Let this mind be in you which was also in Christ Jesus.... He humbled Himself and became obedient to the point of death, even the death of the cross.

—PHILIPPIANS 2:5, 8

Set your mind on things above, not on things on the earth.

—COLOSSIANS 3:2

For God has not given us a spirit of fear, but of power and of love and of a sound mind.

—2 TIMOTHY 1:7

Therefore gird up the loins of your mind, be sober, and rest your hope fully upon the grace that is to be brought to you at the revelation of Jesus Christ.

—1 PETER 1:13

My brother-in-law, Pastor Ronald Scott, has been battling with colon cancer now for nearly three years at this writing. He is a pastor and is truly a mighty man of God. He is like Nathanael, the disciple of whom Jesus said, "Behold, an Israelite indeed, in whom is no deceit!" (John 1:47). I love this man of God for his fervency but most of all for his faith. Since he received the word from the doctors that he had this disease, his faith has never moved. My sister and their children were greatly devastated. As they were leaving the doctor's office that day, he asked my sister and his oldest daughter, "Why are y'all crying? If God is finished with me, then I am ready to go; if He's not finished with me, then I still have work to do. I'm not going anywhere until God is finished with me." Two Christmases have passed since the doctors said he would not make it, and he is still here.

Every time he would have to go in and take some scans or do some tests, as soon as he finished, he would go home immediately. He would not stay for the consultation. He would tell his family,

"I know what they are going to say. I just believe God. When it is my time, then I will go; but until then I am going to keep trusting, believing, pastoring my church, preaching, laying hands on the sick, and watching God do great and mighty things."

That is exactly what he is doing! You might ask, "How in the world is he doing that?" Obviously there is a grace on him right now to walk through this season of his life. There is also an anointing upon him to live this miraculous faith walk daily. And God is keeping His Word. He always will. Ronald prophesies to his body every day, he and his family partake of Holy Communion every day, and they keep faith alive. He is persisting in his persistence.

There is a saying that goes like this: "Persistence is like wrestling with a gorilla. You don't quit when you get tired; you quit when the gorilla gets tired."

I want to prophesy to you right now that I sense in the spirit realm that the gorilla (Satan himself) is getting tired. Did you know that you can wear the enemy down? Did you know that you can frustrate him to a certain point that he and all the little demons will pick up their bags and leave because their efforts are ineffective? Don't believe me? Look at what happened when Jesus came into the place where the demon-possessed man was. Instead of Jesus casting them into the outer darkness and into the eternal abyss, the demons asked to be sent into the pigs. Even the pigs had better sense; they said, "We would rather die than to have these devils living in us."

The demons had to go. They had no choice. This is what I believe is happening in you right now. There is an anointing that is going to hit your life that is going to cause every enemy of your life to go. When you open your mouth and begin to prophesy, change is going to come.

So I say to you again: you are anointed to prophesy to your situation and command it to line up to the living Word of God. If you can *say it* according to God's unchanging, infallible Word, then you will *see it* come to pass!

It's Time!

This takes me back to Ezekiel. The Bible says when he obeyed God and prophesied to those bones, "there was a noise, and suddenly a rattling; and the bones came together, bone to bone" (Ezek. 37:7). I believe that as you believe God and flow in the spirit of prophecy, something is going to start rattling and shaking! The wind of the Spirit is going to start blowing and the power of the anointing is going to be released. I say to you: those *very dry, disjointed bones* in the valley where God has placed you, whatever they may be, are going to *come together* and *come to life* for the glory of God.

Ecclesiastes 3:1 declares, "To everything there is a season, a time for every purpose under heaven." I believe, according to Psalm 102:13, the "set time" has arrived for the people of God. It is time to begin to prophesy to ourselves and our situations... *it is time!* It is time for your breakthrough; it is time for your healing; it is time for your children to be saved and for your marriage to be restored; it is time to get out of debt... to lose weight... to see every prophecy fulfilled in your life that has been declared over you.

When a woman is pregnant, she doesn't have to go around at nine months declaring to everyone, "I'm pregnant!" Everybody she comes in contact with knows she is pregnant. Let's take this a little farther. When things really begin to start happening and she and her husband rush to the hospital and walk up to the front desk, the first thing out of her mouth *is not*, "I'm expecting!" No! She is screaming, her husband is screaming, and if they have other family with them, they are all screaming—"*It's time! It's time!*"

That's what I hear the Holy Spirit confirming in your spirit as you read this book: "*It's time! No more expecting! It's time... now!*" But there are some things you have to do. The first thing you need to do is open your mouth and declare the Word. Prophesy *to yourself* and prophesy over your situation *for yourself.* And sure, get some help if you can. There is power in agreement. But know this: from the beginning of Creation God made sure that you are anointed to prophesy!

Second Corinthians 4:6 says, "For it is the God who commanded light to shine out of darkness, who has shone in our hearts to give the light of the knowledge of the glory of God in the face of Jesus Christ." Jesus, the Word made flesh, lives in you, and His testimony is the spirit of prophecy. I say to you: it is time to believe God, and according to His Word, let the anointing to prophesy flow in and through you. You are anointed for this!

⬭ LET IT BE to ME . . .

When God declared, "Let there be ...," a mighty anointing was released and the host of heaven went to work. When Ezekiel declared life over those dead, dry bones in obedience to God, things started shaking and coming together according to his words.

Friend, the Word of God—Jesus Christ, the Word made flesh—is our final authority. He is the essence of prophecy; He is the demonstration and declaration of God's revealed word. And He lives in you by the power (anointing) of the Holy Spirit. So in the matchless name of Jesus, I say that from a transformed mind you will begin to prophesy the word of the Lord as you go about your everyday life.

Lift your voice right now and begin to prophesy God's sovereign will as revealed in His Word over those "dead things" in your life. Change the atmosphere! Declare to those very dry, disjointed bones: "Hear the word of the Lord. You shall live again!" Go ahead; do it with authority! Do it with confidence! Do it now! It's time! You are anointed to prophesy!

seven

THE WARFARE ANOINTING

The Lord is a warrior; Yahweh is his name.... Your right hand, O Lord, is glorious in power. Your right hand, O Lord, smashes the enemy.... Let us, your servants, see you work again; let our children see your glory. And may the Lord our God show us his approval and make our efforts successful. Yes, make our efforts successful!

—EXODUS 15:3, 6; PSALM 90:16–17, NLT

M IKE MURDOCK HAS said that warfare is proof your enemy has discerned your future.[1] We know that the devil is not omniscient (i.e., all-knowing), but he does have some sort of awareness that God is up to something in your life. The bad news is, "In the world you will have tribulation..." These words are printed in red in the Bible because Jesus spoke them. But He also declared the good news: "...but be of good cheer, I have overcome the world" (John 16:33).

We also know that Jesus came to destroy the works of the devil—so warfare is inevitable! It is going to happen. Someone has wisely said, "If you're not in a battle right now, you have just come through one or you are about to enter one." I know that is not comforting, but it is certainly reality. Warfare is a subject many people don't want to address because they don't like the idea of realizing that they have a real, living, breathing, and engaging enemy. The truth of the matter is, the sooner you realize the devil is always "seeking whom he may devour" (1 Pet. 5:8), the sooner you will realize he is after you; your family; your body and mind; your future, destiny, and purpose; and anything else good that comes from God. And the sooner you will need to come up with a spiritual warfare strategy to defeat him.

I believe this generation is *rising up* and *waking up* to the enemy's schemes, and we are beginning to make this fight fair. Powerful revelations are coming forth and confirmations from the spirit realm are coming to pass before our very eyes—something is definitely changing and moving in the heavenlies! Of course, when we talk about a fight, we already know it really isn't fair, because this fight is fixed! God fixed it a long time ago.

How so? The Bible says Jesus is "the Lamb slain from the foundation of the world" (Rev. 13:8). We also have the anointing to prophesy, which God set in place at the beginning of time. (See Genesis 1:3.) And when the Word of the Lord goes forth, everything in the heavenly and earthly realms—yes, even *very dry bones*—starts shaking! That's right! The Lord is a "man of war" (Exod. 15:3)! As we come to God in true worship, declaring His Word in our anointed praise, prayers, actions, and prophetic declarations, we are declaring all-out war on the enemy. What's more, we have also read the back of the Book! We win here and now, and we win in the age to come! (See Revelation 19–22.) So though the devil fights hard trying to steal, kill, and destroy (John 10:10), as we hold fast our profession of faith, he's fighting a losing battle.

We Must Face and Conquer the Enemy

Even the children of Israel had to face their enemies. After wandering in the wilderness for forty years, when the nation began to inherit the Promised Land, they had to conquer and destroy all of the "ites." Joshua 10:40 says, "So Joshua conquered all the land:

the mountain country and the South and the lowland and the wilderness slopes, and all their kings; he left none remaining, but utterly destroyed all that breathed, as the LORD God of Israel had commanded."

Later, in Joshua 24, Joshua gathered the people in Shechem and reminded them of how God had given them victory over their enemies. Here is the list:

- The Amorites on the other side of the Jordan (v. 8)
- Then after crossing the Jordan, the men of Jericho (v. 11)
- The Perizzites
- The Canaanites
- The Hittites
- The Girgashites
- The Hivites
- The Jebusites

The only exception were the Gibeonites, who deceived the children of Israel by saying they were from a far country and were seeking peace. To Israel's dismay the indictment was that they did not ask for the counsel from the Lord, and as a result, the Gibeonites were not removed from the land. (See Joshua 9:3–21.)

God had ordered Israel to wipe out all of these people groups because of their perversion and idolatry. The land had to be purged, and God expected Israel to actively participate with Him in that process. Though their victories were from the Lord, most of the battles were fought in hand-to-hand and face-to-face combat. Perhaps this is why generations later David could proclaim in the midst of all his victorious battles, "Blessed be the LORD my Rock, who trains my hands for war, and my fingers for battle" (Ps. 144:1).

As we have already seen, David was a true worshipper who prayed, praised, and declared the word of the Lord. God made him a mighty warrior. When David escaped from Saul to the cave of Adullam, God started forming an army to follow him. First Samuel 22:1–2 says, "And when his brothers and all his father's house heard it, they went down there to him. And everyone who was in distress, everyone who was in debt, and everyone who was discontented gathered to him. So he became a captain over them. And there were about four hundred men with him."

In the natural those men had plenty to be discouraged about, but here is what made the difference in their lives—they were in the cave with a *giant killer*. In that cave they all became intimately acquainted with David, and the anointing on David's life rubbed off on each of these men. *Let me tell you something: when they came out of that cave, they were mighty, violent men of war.*

It matters whom you go into battle with. Now, of course, when we are facing battles, the Father, Son, and Holy Spirit are with us. That goes without saying. Yet there are times that I have to make sure there are some Holy Ghost–anointed and –appointed men and women of God in my inner circle, people who know how to be anointed for warfare. These warriors know how to worship, pray, fast, and declare the Word of the Lord. They know how to use their swords to take the heads off of giants.

Believe God and Fight

Several years ago I wrote a book titled *Take It by Force!* In it I challenged the people of God to realize that we have authority and power over the enemy, through the power God has given to us, to take back everything that has been stolen from us. I've said it before, and I'll say it again: the kingdom of heaven suffers violence!

The violent, radical believers from every walk of life take it by force. (See Matthew 11:12.) We can *press in* through warfare prayer and then step out and actively take ground for God's kingdom.

In the previous chapter you read about my brother-in-law, Pastor Ronald Scott, who is a very successful pastor in North Carolina along with his wife, my sister, Alice, and the incredible attack that came into their lives. During the attack that Pastor Scott encountered, my sister began a forty-day journey of prayer and fasting, believing God "until." What does that mean? It means you pray until you see an answer. For forty days and forty nights my sister went without food, sleep, and rest. She got a victory when her husband's cancer went into remission. But after this long, hard battle my sister sank into a deep, dark depression—where she even questioned her salvation. This mighty woman of God, who copastored with her husband at their church and was a Bible teacher, was questioning her very existence as a child of God. The only thing that kept her alive and in faith was her anointing and warfare spirit. She would not give up. She persevered. She fought. She worshipped. And she prayed. Today, five years later, she shares the most incredible journey of coming out of depression that I have ever witnessed. "Now thanks be to God, which always causeth us to triumph in Christ" (2 Cor. 2:14, kjv). My sister has her life, her family, and her ministry back—and her violent faith that nothing can shake.

I say to you: no matter what you are facing—even if you are depressed and distressed, in debt, discontented, or discouraged— you are anointed to be a mighty warrior for God.

Last year an opportunity of a lifetime was presented to me. I was asked to be the special guest of President Yoweri Museveni of Uganda for Uganda's Golden Jubilee. This was a very momentous occasion for me, but it was especially so for this amazing nation, as they were celebrating the victory they won fifty years ago, freeing them from being under British rule. The years they spent under the dictatorship of Idi Amin were considered to be some of the darkest days in the history of this beautiful country.

An interesting side note is that Idi Amin was believed to be cannibalistic.[2] I believe he was the devil himself in the flesh. His tragic story is typical of Satan going about as a roaring lion, "seeking whom he may devour" (1 Pet. 5:8). Just as James 4:7 declares, "Therefore submit to God. Resist the devil and he will flee from you," the people of Uganda did exactly this to get themselves free from Idi Amin. There were at that time, and still are, some powerful prayer warriors who went to work and took back their country in the name of Jesus. Today, thank God, there is Christian government leadership.

For several beautiful days we had an opportunity to celebrate freedom, deliverance, and prosperity with thousands of Ugandans. There in the city of Kampala, Uganda, at the Kololo Ceremonial Ground, thousands of Ugandans thronged the grounds in pomp and circumstance to celebrate the anniversary of a lifetime. The colorful ceremony was attended by more than twenty-two leaders from Africa and other foreign dignitaries from China, Britain, and Italy, to name just a few of the countries represented. Instead of trying to explain all of it, let me give you an example of how one writer captured a moment-by-moment detail of how everything went down:[3]

- 12:10 p.m.: President Museveni takes his seat, as do several other guests in the main pavilion. Well, for the crowd, I think there won't be any sitting for you today.

- 12:11 p.m.: Time for prayers now.

- 12:15 p.m.: The outgoing Archbishop of the Church of Uganda, Henry Luke Orombi, takes the podium first. In his prayer, he says: "We pray for a future where our politics can give hope to the people of Uganda; where Uganda is the head and not the tail."

- 12:20 p.m.: The Mufti of Uganda, Sheikh Shaban Mubajje follows suit. He prays that, "God blesses, guides and protects the leader of Uganda, Yoweri Kaguta Museveni."

- 12:22 p.m.: American gospel singer Judy Jacobs of "The Days of Elijah" fame, is invited to sing exactly what she's popularly known for. This surely ignites the whole of Kololo into some unimaginable spiritual ecstasy. She's really good!

- 12:28 p.m.: Following the brief live performance of Judy Jacobs, there is a march past in slow and quick pace, next on "menu." For now, we start with the slower march.

As you can see, things were pretty much planned to the minutest detail. As I walked to the stage with the other two men, I felt well aware that I was completely out of my league. First, I was a woman who would be onstage with two of the most powerful religious men in the entire country (and who represented other African countries as well). And second, I was a gospel singer from the United States. As l walked on the stage, one of these men caught my eye. To say the least, I was nervous and feeling quite out-of-sorts being on the same stage with these men. Then I had to sing one of the most powerful songs, decreeing and declaring exactly who God Almighty, the Lord God of Abraham, Isaac, and Jacob, is! Singing "Days of Elijah" and declaring "There's NO God like Jehovah!" was beyond my wildest dreams.

As I took the stage, I could see that one of these men looked at me with a piercing eye, as if to say, "What in the world are you doing on this stage beside me? This is not a place for you." I knew that dreadful feeling because l had felt it before and was no stranger to it. Well, to be perfectly honest, that really aggravated me (to say the least). Then I thought, "OK, thank you, devil; that is exactly what I needed."

He was trying to intimidate me. He was trying to get me to think I was less than able to do what God had called me to Uganda to do. That made me really want to sing my song. And sing I did, as you can see from the reporter's notes. I, along with about forty to fifty thousand Ugandans, began to declare out loud, "There's no God like Jehovah!" Let me tell you something: boldness and authority came up within me that can only be described as *violent warfare*!

At that point I didn't care who was onstage, off stage, in the stadium, or most certainly under it! I had the victory, and I declared that song over the nation, its president and first lady, its people, and its land—"There's no God like Jehovah!"

If you are not careful, the devil will always win standoffs. You have to make up your mind, open your mouth, and *say*, "I am going to fight this thing," whatever the "thing" may be. If you go back and forth trying to decide if the struggle you are facing is merely human, or if the enemy is trying to destroy you, a relationship, or a work you are laboring for, then let me help you. *The enemy is trying to destroy you!* You have to believe God and fight every step of the way. You are anointed for this!

Kaylee's Battle

I vividly remember one of the biggest spiritual battles I have encountered so far in my Christian walk. It involved my eldest daughter, Judith Kaylee. She is the precious little baby who came after our first miscarriage, so you can imagine how Jamie and I felt about this tiny "perfect angel." And that is exactly what she is in our lives. Then when her sister, Erica Janell, came along over two years later, my, oh, my! We were really having fun by then.

We noticed something strange beginning to crop up in Kaylee's life when she was around eight years old, and it really started to concern us. She began to be bothered with childhood fears. At first it was as simple as being scared of Disney characters at Disney World, and then it grew to include clowns, dogs, and going downstairs at night by herself. These were just plain and simple things that we would define as the common fears most kids have struggled with. But then her fears began to escalate. She started having nightmares, thinking that she would not live to see the next day.

One time as she toured the Louisville Slugger Museum and Factory in Kentucky, she began to think that she couldn't breathe and that sawdust was going to kill her. As you can imagine, any parent would have been devastated, to say the least, dealing with all of this. But our daughter, our Kaylee? No! This couldn't happen to us, not in a million years. It has been said that your gifts attract attacks. Second Corinthians 2:11 says, "We are not ignorant of his [Satan's] devices." We knew there was an anointing on our child's life, but this fear thing was taking us to a place we had never dreamed was possible. We didn't know what this challenge would turn out to be in the end. I'm going to let Kaylee explain in her own words what this "journey to freedom" was like for her.

> I was born into a family of two passionate people of God. Everyone around me always knew I had an amazing calling on my life, and I was about to find out. When l was about six weeks old, they took me on my first ministry trip to the West Coast in California. My mom was really concerned that I was going to be breathing in all of those people's germs, and she was uptight about it. But I guess she got over it, because that would certainly not be my last trip on an airplane. Growing up in a traveling evangelistic ministry, when I left town I never knew what would be spoken or declared over my life by the powerful men

and women of God we came in contact with. Because as Mom said, "Everyone wanted to see the 'miracle baby.'" Of course, I would never remember what happened, but my mom and dad have always told me about all the things that were prophesied over my life when I was young. But what I'm about to tell you, well, it was one of the best nights of their lives.

I was too young to remember this, but according to my dad, there was a great expectation in the room for God to do something glorious. We were in Albertville, Alabama, and Mom had preached heaven down, and there was a presence in the room that was quite tangible. During the altar call a worship leader was flowing in a prophetic anointing. After about twenty minutes of just worshipping, the minister called my dad out, who was holding me, and he started prophesying over me through a song. In the song he said, "You are holding a prophet. She will prophesy to the nations. She will lay hands on people, and they will be healed and set free of their bondages through the Lord. She will play music and write songs of deliverance." Again, I was just a small child with no concept of what was going on.

Years later, when I was around seven years old, the enemy attacked me with a brutal spirit of fear. It was an experience of total torment for my family and me. I knew I was called to be used by God, but I was struck in such a way that I never thought I would live to prophesy and see miracles, signs, or wonders. It was all I could do to function throughout the day. I remember yelling and screaming at my parents, begging them to help me when I would have anxiety attacks and deep fears. On many occasions my issues totally interfered with Mom and Dad's ministry schedule, and they would have to cancel trips because of "family problems."

Whatever you can imagine about fear while reading this,

I dealt with it. There were days the devil convinced me I would die. He tortured me with crazy, impossible thoughts of failure. Some of the lies were so demonic that I choose not to even share them in this testimony. Every day my parents were there to encourage me, and many times they would tell me, "Kaylee, you are called by God according to His purpose, and the devil hates the anointing on your life." They were constantly, as my mom says, "pleading the blood of Jesus" over my bedroom and everything connected to me. There were many days that Dad would take me to school only to bring me back home, because I was so bound by fear that I couldn't get out of the car. I hated it, but I could not control it—not by myself anyway.

As I lived through this, my grades dropped, I started losing friends, and I couldn't eat. Consequently I lost weight. I could feel myself drifting away from the Lord and feeling that He wasn't anywhere near me. I didn't know it, but my spirit was fighting at all times. My mom had taught me to be a fighter in prayer, so I would pray and quote the scripture for myself over and over again, "God has not given me a spirit of fear, but of power of love and a sound mind" (2 Tim. 1:7). After what seemed like a lifetime—many days of total fasting by my mom and dad; both of them spending countless days in my bed and in my room with a bottle of anointing oil, prayer cloth, and a tallit (a Hebrew prayer shawl); friends and family fasting, pleading the blood of Jesus over my mind and my life—something broke in the spirit realm.

Our family went to The Ramp with Karen Wheaton and Chosen in Hamilton, Alabama, for a kids' crusade, where Minister Becky Fisher was the guest speaker. I was filled with the Holy Spirit. I literally felt the power of God come over me; the spirit of fear left me, and in its place came joy. I left changed and healed *and* delivered. It was the best feeling ever!

During the past few years it has become so obvious why there was such a deadly assault on me at an early age. As you can imagine, my parents were doing anything and everything they could to help me bring change in my life. One day Dad brought home a guitar simply to bring distraction to my thoughts. I didn't know how to play it, but there was something about the guitar that I was attracted to. Not long after, I began to take lessons, playing songs, writing songs, and I even developed the ability to read music. The guitar became my place to run to. I found God's presence there. He would meet me and calm me.

Now, by God's grace, I play in our church (which is another thing the enemy hates), and I help lead worship in our youth meetings. Recently I was privileged to travel with Mom and Dad to Nigeria, and I preached in front of thousands upon thousands of people, giving my testimony and declaring, "You are God's chosen people, and there is no need for you to live in fear either." I began to prophesy revival to them, and the people were blessed...and so was I. I couldn't believe that this was the same girl who couldn't even go into her classroom to face her classmates. And now, *wow*! Look at God!

When I feel and witness the Word of God flowing through me, whether it's through the Word, through a song, or through my guitar—and then I see people's lives changed as a result of my testimony—I now know I was anointed for something great and mighty. Now my prayer is, "Bring it on, Lord! I'm ready and absolutely open to whatever You have for me." Now when the enemy comes in and tries to bring fear, doubt, and unbelief in my life, I just laugh in his face and remind him that he is a liar and that he has no hold on my life anymore. I can tell you by experience that if you will claim this anointing that my mom is writing about, he will have no hold on your life either. Keep the faith. You are anointed for this!

This is an amazing testimony of grace and the power of prayer, and also the triumph in fighting "the good fight of faith" (1 Tim. 6:12). And as you can see, it was a *good fight*, but look what happened: WE WON! Oh, sure, there will be more battles, more warfare, but "the weapons of our warfare are not carnal but *mighty in God* for pulling down strongholds" (2 Cor. 10:4, emphasis added). I'll say it again, according to Matthew 11:12, "The kingdom of heaven suffers violence, and the violent take it by force."

What do we take? We take the kingdom of God *and* the kingdom of darkness all at the same time. As a violent warrior in faith, you do everything that is necessary to *fight the good fight* and *stay in faith*. You are doing kingdom violence! Violent people are focused; they push aside every distraction as they flow in the anointing of the Lord. Read this testimony with me:

My wife, Cheryl, and I have been Christian sojourners our entire adult life. I was raised Roman Catholic and Cheryl, Lutheran and Southern Baptist, and the concept of the anointing was never mentioned or was looked upon with skepticism. It was not until a chance encounter with Perry Stone that we encountered the anointing in a way that changed our lives forever.

The anointing is not something that you need to search for like buried treasure. It is not something that you need to seek and receive, but rather, activate through faith. The anointing defines who you are...it is the "oxygen" in a Christian's life. It sustains us...empowers us...defines us. It is what activates your faith and makes you a "doer" of the word (James 2:14). Without it you are only playing Christian.

There are no excuses...no distinction between those in the pew and those behind a pulpit when it comes to the anointing, either in ability or responsibility. The anointing is what guides and empowers you. It catapults you from "believing" to "knowing." It empowered David to "run" toward Goliath and can empower you to overcome every obstacle in your life as well![4]

—Bob Gesing
Business Entrepreneur/Architect/Minister

I praise God that Kaylee was catapulted to violent faith through the power of the anointing. It literally became the oxygen in her life, and in ours, as we walked through those dark days. What the enemy meant for harm, God has turned around for our good and His glory! I thank Him with every breath that is in me for the warfare anointing.

Put on Your Spiritual Armor

Now let's take a look at the spiritual armor that we activate by faith through the power of the anointing. I have no doubt that the apostle Paul was probably looking right at a first-century Roman soldier when he penned these words:

Therefore take up the whole armor of God, that you may be able to withstand in the evil day, and having done all, to stand. Stand therefore, having girded your waist with *truth*, having put on the breastplate of *righteousness*, and having shod your feet with the *preparation* of the gospel of peace; above all, taking the shield of *faith* with which you will be able to quench all the fiery darts of the wicked one. And take the helmet of *salvation*, and the sword of the Spirit, which is the *word of God*; praying always with all prayer [*proseuche*, pouring out" and supplication [*deesis*, establishing His purposes on earth] in the Spirit, being watchful to this end with all perseverance and supplication for all the saints.

—EPHESIANS 6:13–18, EMPHASIS ADDED

You can't become a mighty warrior without a fight. Remember David's mighty men who started out distressed, in debt, and discontented. When the warfare anointing upon David (the giant killer) came upon them as well, they fought, and won, many battles. They learned how to put on their armor and maintain their weapons. And they took back much ground for what later became David's kingdom. By the power of the Anointed One, a man of war who takes down every enemy, you can get dressed for battle every day and persevere until victory comes.

Ultimately David reigned as king in Judah for seven and a half years, and then over all of Israel for another thirty-three. (See 2 Samuel 5:4–5.) And during his reign the ark of the covenant, which symbolizes the presence and power of God, was returned to Jerusalem (2 Sam. 6:12–19). *Do you get the picture?* Though we may fight many battles, victory is ours! We are anointed for this!

ADVANCE AND TAKE YOUR MOUNTAIN!

Now that we have established some things about the enemy and warfare, where do we fight? "The Seven Mountain Prophecy," declared by men such as the late Bill Bright, Pastor Johnny Enlow, Lance Wallnau, and other men of God, admonishes us that we are called to impact our culture through what they call "The Elijah Revolution" by invading and impacting the seven global areas of society:

1. Media

2. Government

3. Education

4. Economy

5. Religion

6. Celebration/Arts

7. Family

How do we invade each of these seven mountains and impact our culture? In *spirit* and in *truth*! (Go back and read John 4:23.) Remember, God is seeking true worshippers. That means we develop godly character through devotion to the Lord (i.e., spirit) and practical discipline (i.e., truth)—and "basic training" is where we all start.

You see, we are soldiers, not spectators. Worship, praise, prayer, prophesying, and warfare are all *active*. That means every day, because we love God, we discipline ourselves and make seeking God and His kingdom as real as getting up, going to school or work, eating meals, paying our bills, and so on. We submit to God and obey the Holy Spirit, and He brings dynamic change in our lives.

When spirit and truth are in balance in our day-to-day schedules, we stay in the posture to say yes to God and, by the anointing, make a powerful difference in our spheres of influence. Which mountains has God called and gifted you to be a part of? He wants you to show forth His glory by developing exceptional skills and abilities in those areas and by being even more powerful in the Spirit than you are in your natural abilities. As you complete "basic training," God will use you to impact the culture around you by giving you advanced assignments as a seasoned warrior in His kingdom.

Now remember, the enemy does not play fair, nor does he play by the rules. We are involved in a life-and-death struggle; therefore the stakes are enormously high.

Interestingly Scripture tells us, "Submit to God. Resist the devil and he will flee from you" (James 4:7); it doesn't tell us to rebuke the enemy. He, the Lord, rebukes the devourer for our sakes when we submit to His Word (Mal. 3:11). If we are obedient and march to His orders, we will conquer the enemy in our land of promise. God's strategies, His strength, and His supply will give us victory every time.

May we be like Joshua, of whom it was said, "As the LORD had commanded Moses his servant, so Moses commanded Joshua, and so Joshua did. He left nothing undone of all that the LORD had commanded Moses....Not a word failed of any good thing which the LORD had spoken to the house of Israel. All came to pass" (Josh. 11:15; 21:45). And may we be like David, who fought and won many battles until he became king over all Israel. May the warfare anointing be so powerful in your life that you will speak to your mountain, and it will shake and quake just as Zechariah 4:7 declares, "Nothing, not even a mighty mountain, will stand in Zerubbabel's [insert your name here] way; it will become a level plan before him [you]" (NLT). And you will be transformed by the anointing for the glory of God.

YOU CAN FIGHT THE GOOD FIGHT AND WIN!

I read this blog recently:

> With all that is going on in the Middle East, I saw an interesting article in the *Wall Street Journal* while sitting in the Miami airport yesterday. The article was "Israel's Iron Dome Defense Battled to Get Off Ground."
>
> It gave the history of the Iron Dome system and how it came about despite military, political, and monetary resistance. The system went operational in March 2011. During the past two weeks it had knocked down 421 rockets fired from Gaza. Here is what the feat was: "The project's specs demanded a system that could continuously scan all of Gaza,

detect a rocket the instant it was fired, no matter how big or small, pinpoint its likely strike location, and finally, if it was going to hit a city, blast it out of the sky with a missile. The system needed to do all that within about 15 seconds."[5]

Wow! Surely, "Behold, He who keeps Israel shall neither slumber nor sleep" (Ps. 121:4). Friend, let's pray for the peace of Jerusalem and all of Israel according to Psalm 122:6. God has promised that those who love Jerusalem will prosper.

Now I say to you, just like that Iron Dome Defense, the weapons of our warfare are *mighty in God* to the pulling down of strongholds! So let me ask you: *In what condition are your spiritual weapons? In our atomic/information age, are your weapons up-to-date?* As we take on the warfare anointing—worshipping, praising, praying, and prophesying—God gives us spiritual strategies, systems, scanners, and strikers that can take down a supernatural force within seconds of an attack.

May God raise up atomic intercessors who will stand on the wall as watchmen did in the Bible. May He sound the alarm in the spiritual realm and awaken the watchmen in every mountain of society and culture. I pray the warfare anointing of God will strike fear in the enemy's heart, especially in the mountain of government, so our leaders will stand up for righteousness in this nation. Proverbs 14:34 declares, "Righteousness makes a nation great; sin is a disgrace to any nation" (GNT).

And may God stir your spirit so you will rise up in the warfare anointing and take down the schemes of the enemy. As we are obedient, as we keep ourselves consecrated, and as we take our orders from the Lord while warring with His weapons, we will win the war. Someone once said, "Temptation is the tempter looking through the keyhole into the room where you're living. Sin is your drawing back the bolt and making it possible for him to enter."[6]

As a violent warrior in faith you must do everything that is necessary to *stay in faith*. You are doing kingdom violence! Violent warriors are focused, and they push aside every distraction. We don't throw in the towel, and we don't quit—*because quitting is not an option!* You have a warrior's anointing, an undeniable unction from the Holy One, and you must refuse to be denied. So gird yourself up in spirit and in truth and fight! You are anointed to engage in battle and prevail—for your children, your marriage, your body, your mind, and in every area of life. *Don't ever forget: you are anointed for this!* So fight the good fight, because *we win!*

⌒ LET IT BE to ME . . .

I declare to you there is no God like Jehovah! He is a man of war! His right hand is glorious in power, and He dashes the enemy in pieces. But He expects us to actively participate with Him in battle.

As you advance in your calling and purpose, you must know that warfare is inevitable…because you are a soldier in God's kingdom like David, Joshua, and many others who have gone before you. There is a mighty warfare anointing inside of you! You can fight and *win*, knowing God has already set the odds in your favor.

Now let me ask you: Are you struggling against a spiritual attack as Kaylee was? Has the enemy launched an all-out ambush, trying to keep you bound so he can choke the anointing in your life?

If you have been struggling in a particular area and can't seem to get the victory, get godly agreement. Go to a leader, a mentor, or a friend or family member—someone who takes the kingdom by force and won't be denied. I say to you that the yoke of the enemy will be broken off of your life by the power of the Anointed One! I declare you will rise up in spirit and in truth, put on your armor, and take your mountains for the glory of God. *You are anointed for this!*

eight

THE UNCTION *to* FUNCTION

Now, dear brothers and sisters, regarding your question about the special abilities the Spirit gives us.... There are different kinds of spiritual gifts, but the same Spirit is the source of them all. There are different kinds of service, but we serve the same Lord. God works in different ways, but it is the same God who does the work in all of us.

—1 Corinthians 12:1, 4–6, NLT

T HE "UNCTION TO function" is a catchy little phrase, but more than that, it is a phrase explaining what you will need in the spirit realm in order to carry out your assignment or requirement that is expected of you. It also speaks of the Holy Spirit's power to work within you, allowing you to operate in a realm of glory you have never operated in. Now, if we were totally transparent, we would admit that we want to constantly be changing "from glory to glory" in our walk with the Lord (2 Cor. 3:18). We don't ever want to become stagnant and dormant. We want to constantly move with the cloud of God's glory and presence, under the power of the anointing, to function in the capacity He has gifted us for.

Dr. Shirley Arnold, pastor of Epic Church in Lakeland, Florida, says, "The anointing is God's enablement to accomplish His purpose on this earth. It is our privilege to be vessels of His anointing.

Just as Jesus was anointed with the Holy Spirit to do great miracles, we must be anointed to do His works. The anointing is the 'X Factor.' It moves a desire into a reality. It activates a dream into a fulfillment. It captures disappointment and bursts forth in hope. It transforms fear into the boldness of a lion!"[1]

Think of it this way. From before you were born God loved you and had a purpose for your life. So He sent the anointing, and you called upon His name to be saved. Then He released His anointing again, and you took the next step in your walk with Him. Every time you have advanced in your Christian life, from glory to glory, it has been because you responded to the Holy Spirit's unction to function.

I'm not talking about you coming up with a good plan or idea. I'm talking about that "X Factor"...when the Lord comes alongside of you and gives you that "spiritual poke" or unction from the Holy One. You know, that tug in your heart that's wrapped in peace, giving you a "knowing" and a desire to do something that you probably hadn't even thought of. God releases His anointing through this unction to function so we will flow in our gifts, talents, and abilities and get kingdom results. And as we obey, in return we see the world being changed for the glory of God. That's what it's all about.

In his book *Radical Together* David Platt realizes, "...the same potential resides in the church in my context. God has given great grace...vast resources, varied gifts, innumerable skills, immeasurable talents, and billions of dollars....If we were willing to alter our lifestyles, and if we were willing to organize our churches around taking the gospel to people who have never heard of Christ, we could see every people group on the planet reached with the gospel."[2]

This is what we are endeavoring to do at our church, Dwelling Place Church International. We are a giving, loving, leading church, and we are also a sending church, releasing people to the uttermost parts of the earth—to Nigeria, Mexico, Uganda, Turkey, Mozambique, Honduras, Colombia, Malawi, Argentina, Russia, and on and on. A mighty unction is upon us, so we continue to go and do greater works in obedience to the Lord. We keep placing a demand on the anointing, tapping the source of the many gifts, ministries, and resources that are in our local body. And this same unction is for the body of Christ at large. To reach the ends of the earth, laboring together under a mighty anointing, we must all yield to the Lord's unction to function.

THE FUNCTION OF THE DIVINE UNCTION

As we are discovering, the anointing is so important in our everyday lives. Let's do a little review and take it from there. In chapter 2 we learned that the word *anointing* comes from the Hebrew root word *anoint*, which generally means to be set apart for God's purpose. This has the same meaning as the word *sanctify*, which means, "to make holy; consecrate."[3]

We also understand from that chapter that the word *unction* is actually a functional part of the word *anointing*. It is part of that "consecratory gift" God gives us to do His work.[4] Now let's look a little deeper. This very interesting word also appears in the New Testament. First John 2:20 says, "But ye have an unction from the Holy One, and ye know all things" (KJV). The word *unction* in this verse is from the Greek word *chrisma* (pronounced khris'-mah). It speaks of "the special endowment ('chrism') of the Holy Spirit."[5] This is also described as "the all-efficient means of enabling believers to possess a knowledge of the truth."[6]

In the modern vernacular the word *unction* is defined as, "an affected or excessive earnestness in manner or utterance."[7] This is something of a motivational word. So what we must realize is that the *unction,* the "motivating force" of God, is His anointing. Look at it like this:

- If you don't sense an anointing to preach, your preaching will be boring.

- If you don't sense an anointing to study, your study will hit and miss.

- If you don't sense an anointing to sing, it will not bless you, and it won't bless others. This is simply true because if you're not blessed by what you do, you won't bless anyone else.

There has to be an unction to function, or a motivating force, that releases the gifts and callings of God in your life. And He is the one who gives you that motivation, that "Giddy up and go!" to get His work done. There have been many times when I was sitting on the front row of a church or standing behind a curtain getting ready to minister in a huge arena or on television, and I didn't feel anything but exhaustion, anxiety, or sheer "I want my mama."

But the moment that I went up on the platform or came from behind the curtain, every single time, there was always an unction to function from the Holy One. Suddenly I was embraced by an anointing to sing that made singing easy, or touched by an anointing to preach that made preaching easy. The best way I can understand when this happens is that I know God is giving me a supernatural ability to do what I am called to a particular place to do.

Being inundated by the anointing helps make my travels pleasant. A divine unction is always present when I leave my husband and children to go minister. I get the unction to function anytime I leave the comfort of the familiar and go to a place, territory, or nation that is unknown to me. Oh, yes! The *unction* is the motivating force of God, the anointing to get things done!

THE UNCTION OF GOD IS YOURS, MINE, AND OURS

In a year's time I do a lot of traveling across this nation and the nations of the earth. Many of the places I go are very exciting. There are also some not-so-exciting places. I will tell you my most favorite places to go and visit are the ones that absolutely put a demand on the anointing inside of me. Usually these are the places where every piece of clothing on my body is soaked with perspiration when I leave.

When this happens, I know the reason: somebody caught a taste of the anointing on my life, and they wanted an impartation of what is inside of me. Now, I didn't say they wanted *my anointing,* because my anointing is just that: the anointing God gives to me. Your anointing is the unique unction and expression God gives to you.

Sometimes people will say to me, "Sister Judy, I want your anointing." My response is always, "No, you don't want my anointing. You want the anointing God has for you. Now, you may desire an impartation from me, but you can't have my anointing, just like I can't have Joyce Meyer's anointing. She is anointed specifically for the calling that is on her life, and I am anointed for the special calling on my life...and so are you."

I don't have my mom's anointing; I have an impartation from my mom, but the unique anointing on my life came from God *to* and *for* me. Remember, God's anointing is *His anointing!* He decides who receives His gifts, when and where we receive them, and how we each flow in His anointing. Why? We have a world to reach for the glory of God. We have a lot of work to do. We need His unction, His motivation, to get going and to complete what He calls us to do.

My friend Karen Wheaton says this about the anointing:

For me, the anointing is a precious treasure. An invaluable gift. My Helper. The source of my confidence. The One who pours through a yielded, ordinary vessel and makes His glorious presence tangible. I was eleven years old the first time I experienced what I know now to be "the anointing." I was singing a song with the children's choir called "There's Something About That Name." I was given a part to speak in the middle of the song, and as I was speaking, suddenly I sensed the Helper. Someone besides me was speaking through me. It was my body, my mouth, my voice, but His Spirit. I felt an empowerment that transcended my age and limitations. I could see the effect of His presence on the listeners. I remember thinking, "Whatever this is, I want it for the rest of my life."[8]

As I said earlier, the anointing you receive from the Father is distinctly yours and yours alone. Yet the same Holy Spirit endows all of God's children with this phenomenal gift. It's a paradox but one that is powerfully effective.

My daughters don't have either my or their daddy's anointing. They have the anointing that God has gifted to them. Now, does it matter that they have been around us all of their lives? Most certainly! They have definitely received an impartation from us, but that doesn't mean we have been trying to reproduce "little Jamies" and "little Judys." Absolutely not.

Over the years I have learned something powerful about the unction to function. Not only does it move each of us to do the work of God, but also it moves in and among us, quickening us to get things done together. If I get around Pastor Rod Parsley, I will experience a Pentecostal fire such as Lester Sumrall and Smith Wigglesworth experienced. This anointing was imparted and passed on to Pastor Parsley by these two men. If I get around Marilyn Hickey, I will gain a love for memorizing the Word of God and a love for missions.

And if I get around Bishop Jakes, I will get loosed! Whom you are around and the impartation they carry definitely make a difference.

So when you place a demand on the anointing upon somebody's life, you are saying in essence, "Whatever is in you, I want to see it come out in me." You are saying to God, "I want to draw from Your power, Lord. I want to see the manifestation of what You are going to do through me, as You're doing through this person," whether it is a speaker, worship leader, psalmist, musician, or whomever the anointing is flowing through at that moment.

For example, when people filled up tents and auditoriums across America to see and hear people like A. A. Allen, Kathryn Kuhlman, Oral Roberts, T. L. Lowery, and many others, they would go expecting to see miracles, signs, and wonders. In those services during that era a demand was put upon these mighty men and women of God for the supernatural. People did not leave disappointed, because God did great and mighty things! Praise God, He is still doing the great and the mighty because He has called us to do greater works! We as the body of Christ must continue to put a demand on the true apostles, prophets, evangelists, pastors, and teachers of our day. One of these true servants of God, Pastor Rod Parsley of World Harvest Church, writes:

> Isaiah 10:27 says, "And it shall come to pass in that day, that his burden shall be taken away from off thy shoulder, and his yoke from off thy neck, and the yoke shall be destroyed because of the anointing."
>
> The anointing is the power of God at work in your life to remove burdens and destroy yokes. The anointing is tangible, therefore it is transferable. The woman with the issue of blood discovered this when she touched the border of Jesus' garment and was made whole. This same anointing resided in Moses' rod, in Elisha's bones, in Peter's shadow and in Paul's handkerchiefs and aprons. Jesus said He was

anointed to preach, to heal, to deliver, and to set free—and so are you.

The first time I experienced the anointing of God was in 1979 in Indianapolis, Indiana. I prayed for a woman whose jaw was horribly deformed, and with a noise like a pistol shot it immediately straightened and became normal. Since that time, I have seen incredible things happen as a result of the anointing, which always comes to set the captives free from whatever has them bound.[9]

Wow! God releases His unction, and when we obey and flow in the anointing, miracles happen! God is still in the miracle-working business! And as we allow Him to move in, among us and through us, there will be no limits to what He will do as we continue the work of Jesus, *preaching the gospel to the poor, healing the broken-hearted, proclaiming liberty to the captives and recovery of sight to the blind,* and *setting at liberty those who are oppressed.* I say to you: God has a lot of work for you to do. Are you ready to obey God and use the supernatural gifts He's given you when He releases His unction in your spirit? I urge you to say yes to the Lord.

THE UNCTION KEEPS GROWING...

Several years ago I felt led to begin a season of fasting and prayer. It was a very strategic time when I needed to see God start to do something greater in my life. I was praying fervently for a stronger anointing. I will never forget it.

During that time, as I was up ministering the word of the Lord, something like a strong wind flew by me, and then something began to happen to my mind and my tongue at the same time. I was amazed at the things that were coming out of my mouth. I would say something, and the moment the words came out, I would think, "Lord, where did that come from?" Finally God spoke to me and said, "This is the new and fresh anointing you have been seeking

Me about and I am placing on you, and that is what it feels like, sounds like, and looks like. Now ask Me, and I will give you more." Since that time I have never looked back, and the anointing on my life has continued to increase because I am never satisfied. I want everything that God has for me and more.

As we keep seeking Him, the demand for the anointing continues expanding in our lives. One thing I have noticed in pursuing God is the moment when I feel that I have "arrived" in my spiritual walk or that I have reached a point when I am just shy of touching Him, God moves on me and whispers, "That's it; come on up a little higher and higher." Now I've come to realize that I will never reach that stature with Him. He is always going to move on me with "greater," and I wouldn't have it any other way.

I pray this same unction upon your life. I pray that, just as people like myself, Rod Parsley, Kathryn Kuhlman, and others have put a demand on the anointing, and our gifts have been tapped as a result of that demand, that you will experience this divine unction to function and do mighty works for God. We are all part of the same team, and God wants to use all of us to get His works done. In fact, the anointing only increases when we work together.

Here's another example. In football there are eleven players who are on the playing field at any one time, but there are more than eleven on the field when you factor in the crowd. The crowd puts a demand on the players to perform.

In Seattle, Washington, the football team is the Seattle Seahawks. Their stadium is called CenturyLink Field, and if you have ever been there, you probably could see why this field is considered one of the loudest stadiums in football. The way the stadium is built and shaped creates a sound vacuum that dominates the environment. The sound is so loud that the opposing team is not able to hear the strategy plays. In the NFL the Seattle Seahawks' "twelfth man" is the most powerful crowd noise in the entire league—because they are the loudest, most boisterous, and most dominating fans against their opponents throughout all four quarters of the game.

I believe in this final hour God is going to send you "cheerleaders" who are going to cheer you on, both in your walk and in your ministry for the kingdom. Their only job will be to encourage you, lift you up, and spur you on in your anointings and giftings. I also believe that the cheers are going to be so overbearing that the enemy will not be able to decipher what God is saying and doing in our lives because of our high praises.

Perhaps our "home crowd" is what the writer of Hebrews was referring to when he wrote:

> Therefore we also, since we are surrounded by so great a cloud of witnesses, let us lay aside every weight, and the sin which so easily ensnares us, and let us run with endurance the race that is set before us, looking unto Jesus, the author and finisher of our faith, who for the joy that was set before Him endured the cross, despising the shame, and has sat down at the right hand of the throne of God.
>
> —Hebrews 12:1–2

Writing from Rome, the author would have been aware of the huge crowds that gathered at the Colosseum to watch sporting events.

What I am talking about is not spooky. When we hunger and thirst for more of God, then He will not disappoint us. I am not talking about a controlled or manipulated environment. I am talking about a spiritual ambience, or even a raw emotion, that will not settle for anything less than God Himself. That kind of audience or congregation will literally pull from the anointing. The anointing, the unction to function, is the unseen force, impetus, or stimulus in ministry! May God increase your hunger for Him and give you a mighty unction to do greater works in this final hour.

THE UNCTION KEEPS YOU GOING

There will be times in your walk with God when you need a touch from Him to keep on going. When this happens, don't condemn yourself. The Lord is very skilled at releasing His special abilities in us. He knows how to work in different ways to get things done. We just need to be obedient to Him as He releases His unction and leads the way. Let's look at a few stories from the Bible to see how God operates.

After the death of Moses God commissioned Joshua. In a point-blank way the Lord said to Joshua, "Moses My servant is dead. Now therefore, arise, go over this Jordan, you and all this people, to the land which I am giving to them—the children of Israel. Every place that the sole of your foot will tread upon I have given you, as I said to Moses" (Josh. 1:2–3). Notice that God didn't say, "Moses My servant has expired." Neither did he say, "Moses My servant is no longer with us." He said point-blank, and I paraphrase, "He is dead. Now get these people to the land that I have promised, and just as I was with Moses, I will be with you."

There was a power unction, a motivation, in God's words that imparted an ability and confidence in Joshua to do what He was appointing him to do. "The pity party is over," God was saying, "Now let's go!" Thus Joshua received the unction to lead the people, and he obeyed the Lord. Joshua led the children of Israel under a mighty anointing for more than twenty-five years.

As I write, I sense an unction that this is what God is saying to you. Someone or something has died. It may have been a spouse, a child, a marriage, a business, a dream, a friend, or even your ministry. But God is saying, "Get up! It's time! You are anointed for this! I'm going to be a friend who will stick closer to you than a brother."

Friend, you can know that even if your mother and father or someone else dear to you forsakes you, the Lord will lift you up. It's time to declare to yourself, "I have been down too long; it's time to move on with the plan that God has for me." Even now you're getting an unction from the Holy One. You already feel a stirring in your spirit...things are changing!

Now let's take a look at how God moved upon the prophet Isaiah. The sixth chapter of the Book of Isaiah opens with him saying, "In the year that King Uzziah died, I saw the Lord sitting on a throne, high and lifted up, and the train of His robe filled the temple" (v. 1). Now, to see the real significance of what Isaiah was saying, it is important to consider the reign of Uzziah in totality:

- Uzziah began his reign at only sixteen years of age.

- He reigned for fifty-two years.

- He was a good and strong king who led Israel to many military victories.

- He was an energetic builder and planner.

- He suffered a tragic end.

So when Isaiah wrote that he was called "in the year that King Uzziah died," he was saying a lot. On an emotional level this verse could read, "In the year our great and wise king died..." But even better, it could say, "In the year our great and wise king who had a tragic end died..." Isaiah had great reason to be discouraged and disillusioned at the death of King Uzziah. This once great king had passed away, and his life had ended tragically. Yet despite it all, God released His unction to Isaiah, and he saw the Lord God enthroned—the King who was greater than any earthly king.

God knew what Isaiah needed to keep going, and He knows exactly what you need. That's why you're reading this book. So rise up; get up! God is with you. He will give you the unction to function again, because as long as you have breath, you have a purpose in God. Say to yourself, "I'm going to see the Lord in this situation. Things might look bad right now, but the things that are seen are only temporary; they are subject to change. The things that are not seen are eternal." Now open your mouth and declare, "I'm getting ready to see the eternal promises of God fulfilled in my life."

We also see this unction to function in the life of Samuel. After the Philistines had defeated the children of Israel and taken the ark of the covenant, bad things began to happen to them. So they sent the ark back to the Israelites. Conversely, everywhere the ark went in Israel, that area was blessed. After suffering defeat, the Israelites were ready to listen to Samuel and repent. Then at the precise time they were gathering together to admit their sins against the Lord, the Philistines decided to attack once again. That's when the unction of the Lord came upon Samuel, and he rose up and offered a burnt offering to God. At the exact time he did this, "the LORD thundered with a loud thunder upon the Philistines that day, and so confused them that they were overcome before Israel" (1 Sam. 7:10).

Fast-forward a few years. Samuel was lamenting that Saul, Israel's king (whom he had anointed), had been rejected by the Lord. God spoke to Samuel and said, "How long will you mourn for Saul, seeing I have rejected him from reigning over Israel? Fill your horn with oil, and go; I am sending you to Jesse the Bethlehemite. For I have provided Myself a king among his sons" (1 Sam. 16:1).

As Samuel saw Jesse's first son, he thought he was surely seeing the Lord's anointed. But remember, the anointing does *not* depend on the flesh. Thankfully Samuel was sensitive to the voice of God. He did not depend on what "seemed" to be right concerning the Lord's anointed. God explained to Samuel, "For the LORD does not see as man sees; for man looks at the outward appearance, but the LORD looks at the heart" (v. 7).

The process continued, and after seven sons of Jesse appeared, there was no divine unction. So Samuel told Jesse that the Lord had not chosen any of them. Then God released His unction, and Samuel asked if Jesse had any more sons. Jesse replied, "There remains yet the youngest, and there he is, keeping the sheep" (v. 11). As David came in, the Lord said to Samuel, "'Arise, anoint him; for this is the one!' Then Samuel took the horn of oil and anointed him in the midst of his brothers; and the Spirit of the LORD came upon David from that day forward" (vv. 12–13).

The Bible says, "We know in part and we prophesy in part," and that one day we will know as we are known (1 Cor. 13:9, 12). So we *must* obey the unction of the Lord to move in the anointing: *when, where,* and *how* God desires. Our response, at the moment God moves in us, determines if we will hit or miss the mark of our calling in Jesus Christ. Paul wrote to the Philippians:

> I focus on this one thing: Forgetting the past and looking forward to what lies ahead, I press on to reach the end of the race and receive the heavenly prize for which God, through Christ Jesus, is calling us.
> —PHILIPPIANS 3:13–14, NLT

The unction of the Lord moved mightily in David's life. I've talked a lot about David because he lived an exceptional life. His reign during the period of Israel's kings proved to be the pinnacle of the nation's history. As I've said already, David was a man after God's own heart and a mighty man of war—yet he was an anointed worshipper.

While David was still a young man, God's unction came upon him, and he played anointed music that relieved King Saul when he was distressed by a tormenting spirit (1 Sam. 16:23). But after David killed Goliath, a jealous spirit overtook Saul; another time while David was playing music for him, Saul threw a spear at him (1 Sam. 18:10–11). But the Word says, "David behaved wisely in all his ways, and the LORD was with him" (v. 14).

The unction to function was so strongly upon David that Saul was afraid of him, "because the LORD was with him, but had departed from Saul" (v. 12). David's life is an excellent example of what walking in the Spirit, in obedience to the unction of the Lord, is all about. Because God had an awesome purpose for David's life, He gave David the unction, again and again, to move forward in faith under a mighty anointing.

As king, David was prolific in worship. He wrote many psalms as he worshipped the Lord. In fact, when the ark was returned to Jerusalem, David moved in the anointing and danced before the Lord with all his might. However, when his wife Michal (Saul's daughter), voiced her contempt over his exuberant worship, he replied, "It was before the LORD" (2 Sam. 6:21). And what happened after this? David remained blessed by the Lord and Michal remained barren (v. 23). I believe she was barren, not because she had been cursed by God, but because David didn't have anything to do with her after that little incident. He chose to put God first in his life, and he wasn't going to let anything dictate his worship, especially his heathen wife.

We also see New Testament saints acting under the unction of the Lord. For example, Peter, who was in Christ's inner circle, denied Him three times on the night He was betrayed (Mark 14:66–72). Then after the Lord was raised from the dead by the power of the anointing, He asked Peter three times, "Do you love Me?" (See John 21:15–17.) That was an unction Jesus used to get Peter to start functioning again. If you remember, Peter preached the sermon on the Day of Pentecost, which resulted in over three thousand souls coming into the kingdom (Acts 2:14–41).

Another time, when Peter and John were on their way to the temple at the hour of prayer, a crippled man asked them for money. Peter stopped, under the unction of the Lord, and "fixing his eyes on him" said to the lame man, "Silver and gold I do not have, but what I do have I give you: In the name of Jesus Christ of Nazareth, rise up and walk" (Acts 3:1–6). Then the anointing went to work and a miracle took place. As the story goes, Peter took him by the right hand and lifted him up, and immediately he was healed. The Bible says that man leaped, walked, and went into the temple with them, praising God (vv. 7–8).

If I were to write about every time the unction to function came upon the people of God, I'd have to write several more books at the very least! Why? After Jesus rose from the dead, before He went to sit at the right hand of the Father in heaven, John 21:25 declares, "And there are also so many other things that Jesus did, which if they were written one by one, I suppose that even the world itself could not contain the books that would be written." He did those things in the span of forty days (Acts 1:3). More than two thousand years have passed since that time, and in my life alone Jesus has done so many great things, I would be pressed to write about them all.

Oh, yes! As Amanda said in chapter 3, the anointing of God, the unction to function, "is a continual flow that does not run out; it cannot be exhausted"! The ups and downs of life can't hinder the flow. The passage of time can't stop it. A broken heart, spirit, or body can't keep it from moving you to do the works of God. Why? Because the anointing is making sure we walk in God's purpose, "…to preach the gospel to the poor…to heal the broken-hearted…to proclaim liberty to the captives and recovery of sight to the blind, to set at liberty those who are oppressed; to proclaim the acceptable year of the LORD" (Luke 4:18–19).

THE KEY CONDITION OF THE LORD'S UNCTION

I know a man in ministry who used to be a missionary to the Pygmy tribes in Dutch New Guinea. After preaching one night through his interpreter, he decided to conduct a healing line. When he noticed the first man in the line had a fungus from head to toe, he changed his mind. In that part of the jungle that particular fungus was highly contagious. So the missionary went back to his tent.

After two hours he looked out; no one had moved. They were all still waiting in the healing line. Feeling chastened by the Lord (a divine unction), he decided to go and minister to the people and just believe God. As he approached the "fungus" man, he used his two pointing fingers only to barely touch the sides of the man's head where there was the least fungus. Then the anointing kicked in. When he touched him, the fungus man leaped onto him and held him: his legs wrapped around his waist and his arms wrapped around his neck.

The missionary described the man as having fungus in his eyes, in his mouth, and all over his body. However, when the power of God touched him through that missionary, praise God, the man was instantly healed.

Obedience is the key for functioning in the anointing. It was the final factor that led to the downfall of King Saul. In 1 Samuel 13:8–15 Saul became impatient and took it upon himself to make a sacrifice rather than wait for Samuel to arrive. Some of Saul's men had already begun to defect. When Samuel arrived, Saul said, in his own defense, that he "felt *compelled*" to do what he did (v. 12, emphasis added). That is the negative side of an "unction to function": doing what seems right to you without the anointing. Samuel rebuked Saul, telling him that he had acted foolishly and had not kept the commandment of the Lord. *Listen: the main rule for having authority is also to be under authority yourself, and that starts with being obedient to the Lord.*

Even Jesus remarked that He had not found such great faith in Israel when He encountered the centurion in Matthew 8. When Jesus told him that He would come and heal his servant, the centurion humbly said, "Lord, I am not worthy that You should come under my roof. But only speak a word and my servant will be healed." He continued, "For I also am a man under authority, having soldiers under me. And I say to this one, 'Go,' and he goes; and to another, 'Come,' and he comes; and to my servant, 'Do this,' and he does it" (vv. 8–9). Now, that is a true picture of *meekness*, a gentle humility that demonstrates power under control.[10]

Going back to Saul, the final blow came when he disobeyed the word of the Lord spoken through Samuel to utterly destroy the Amalekites (1 Sam. 15:1–3). Saul was instructed to attack King Agag and the Amalekites and not to spare anything alive: "Kill both man and woman, infant and nursing child, ox and sheep, camel and donkey" (v. 3). But Saul spared the best the Amalekites had, including the king himself. He then told Samuel "the people" had saved the animals to sacrifice (vv. 9, 13–15). In rebuke, Samuel said, "Has the LORD as great delight in burnt offerings and sacrifices, as in obeying the voice of the LORD? Behold, to obey is better than sacrifice, and to heed than the fat of rams. For rebellion is as the sin of witchcraft" (vv. 22–23). That very day the Lord tore the kingdom of Israel away from Saul (v. 28).

Friend, the unction to function in the anointing of God works within the framework of obedience. God is more interested in our character than our comfort. He is raising up a generation that will *do what He says* in the *correct way*, which will achieve His objective and bring glory to Him—not build up our own egos.

In these last days we must be people and ministers of integrity, honesty, and humility. We must go beyond just knowing the principles of the kingdom; we must also know the King—His will, His ways…His very heartbeat. And again, this is possible because we have "an *unction* from the Holy One, and ye know all things" (1 John 2:20, KJV). The Lord Himself enables us to possess a knowledge of the *truth*, because He is the living Word.

Daniel 11:32 declares, "The people who know their God shall be strong, and carry out great exploits." So let's function in the anointing with the right spirit and with power from on high: God's "X Factor," the unction to function that moves us to obey Him and release a mighty anointing in the earth. Never forget! You are anointed to flow in special abilities that have been tailor-made for you by the same God who does the work in all of us. You can obey God and move in the anointing, whether you are laboring alone or working together with your brothers and sisters in Christ. You can hear, obey, and flow in the anointing of God—fearlessly, favorably, and fiercely. *You are anointed for this!*

⌒ LET IT BE to ME…

God gives us a holy unction to function, so we will move forward in His timing, in His way, to get His results. The unction is God's motivating force to get us to *act* in obedience to His Word. With this in mind, what special abilities has the Lord given you? When He gives you the unction to function in these giftings, do you immediately obey Him? And when the Lord moves you to flow in the anointing with your brothers and sisters in Christ, do you work together with them in a spirit of unity, or do you have problems cooperating with others and/or being under spiritual authority?

Take a few moments now to prayerfully consider how you allow the Lord's unction to function to govern your spiritual walk. Make sure to thank Him for the special gifts

He has given you to serve Him and advance His kingdom. And repent to the Lord for any time you have resisted the Holy Spirit and quenched the anointing. God has great plans for you as you walk in His purpose for your life. I declare to you now that you can know your God and do mighty exploits, because His "X Factor" is within you, ready to be released. *I say to you in the name of Jesus: you are anointed for this!*

nine

THE ANOINTING *to* CHANGE
SOCIETY *and* CULTURE

For God so loved the world that He gave His only begotten Son, that
whoever believes in Him should not perish but have everlasting life.

—JOHN 3:16

T HE TWENTY-FIVE WORDS in the verse you just finished
reading are the central theme of the Bible. I guess you could
call them God's "divine mission statement," His stated purpose for sending Jesus to fulfill His plan of redemption. John 3:16
is what the anointing is all about. It is why God brings us into His
kingdom and begins leading us through a "this" to get us to a "that."
This short verse is the purpose behind every Holy Spirit–breathed
unction to function that has ever been known to man.

God is pouring out His Spirit for a very specific reason: souls—
people just like you and me. Oh, yes! *This* is *that* which was spoken
by the prophet Joel...for such a time as this! God wants to pour
out His power through you not only to change you but also to help
you create a new atmosphere—the atmosphere of the anointing—
to change the culture around you, because His anointing destroys
every yoke of bondage.

John 3:16 is also why the devil doesn't want you to know you are
anointed. He doesn't want you to know your God, discover who

you are in Christ, and, as a mighty warrior in the Spirit, do greater works in the name of Jesus to expand the kingdom. He will try to do anything to distract you from our corporate calling that you read about in the beginning of chapter 3, which just happens to share the title of this book: *You Are Anointed for This!*

> "Go therefore and make disciples of all the nations, baptizing them in the name of the Father and of the Son and of the Holy Spirit, teaching them to observe all things that I have commanded you; and lo, I am with you always, even to the end of the age." Amen.
>
> —Matthew 28:19–20

God Is Building His Character in You

It has been wisely said, "It only takes a few brief words to enter the married life, but it will take thousands of confessions of love through word and action to live the married life." Similarly we enter the Christian life by faith in Jesus Christ and by confessing Him as Lord and Master of our lives—but it takes all of our remaining days to live out our confession daily through our words and deeds. This reminds me of the words of H. Jackson Brown Jr., the *New York Times* best-selling author of *Life's Little Instruction Book*: "Our character is what we do when we think no one is looking."[1]

We are the change agents for what God wants to do on this earth to bring real and lasting change until Jesus comes back to take dominion. What will it take in the meantime to change our society and culture? God is ushering in the greatest revival the world has ever seen, and if Jesus tarries, this will take time. And this is where godly character is tested. Too many people think *time* is a dirty word, just like the word *patience,* or how about this word, *work.* Just as applying these three things builds lasting marriages, it will take all three, applied daily, for the body of Christ to change a society that is messed up, confused, and desperate, simply because people need their Savior.

But in order to get this world healed, many Christians have to get healed themselves. We can't lift someone else up until we get lifted up, and sometimes *the lift you need* is as close as the lift *that you give to someone else.* I have found that when I have been overwhelmed and down in my life, the moment I get my eyes off of "me, me, me" and turn my thoughts to someone else who is worse off than I am, that is the moment when things shift for me. Oh, and by the way, someone else is always worse off than you are. Just take a good look around you, and you will see.

One of the things that can help you to heal and find your meaning, purpose, and destiny—the real reason for your existence and why God brought you here to this planet at this time to do whatever He has specifically called you to do—is prayer. You have to seek the Lord to discover the real reason you were born, why you were born where you were born, to the parents you were born to. You must seek Him to discover the reason God made *you, you*!

Have you ever bought a book not because of its title but because of its subtitle? Publishing companies have people in place to help work through the process of marketing, coming up with unique features and strategies, to help you work through a title, but they especially focus on the subtitle of a book. Subtitles are very important because they take the guesswork out of understanding a book's message. Subtitles break books down to their truest, simplest form.

One such book is *The Purpose Driven Life,* written by Pastor Rick Warren. It has sold more than thirty million copies.[2] In all actuality, the title of the book is not what sold the book. The subtitle got everyone's attention. It poses the question, "What on Earth Am I Here For?" This is the heart cry of every person alive. At the end of the day this is what we all as human beings long to know—that is, to understand, grasp, pursue, and obtain.

Are You Really "Walking the Walk"?

One weekend I was scheduled to minister in San Antonio, Texas. It was right before the Thanksgiving holiday, and the whole downtown area was decorated with all the wonderful things that speak of Christmas for a family to enjoy, particularly for the kids. One of my most favorite spots in San Antonio is the historic River Walk. As usual, the whole downtown area was beautifully decked out with decorations for the Christmas holidays, and there were people galore. I was very happy to have my husband and girls with me. It was a very busy weekend. We had teamed up with a local pastor to distribute brand-new clothes and toys to children of single parents, and the next day I would minister in three services: two in the morning and one in the evening.

On purpose we flew out late on Monday evening because there was a large mall across the street from the hotel where we were staying. As a family we had decided to do some early Christmas shopping. As you can imagine, we were all tired from shopping and ready to go home when the time came for our flight. The flight schedule put us getting into Hartsfield-Jackson Atlanta International Airport around 11:00 p.m., that is, if all went well and everything was on time. After arriving and getting our luggage, we would still have another two hours to drive before getting home.

So we had a little journey ahead of us before we even got started. Unbelievably, we got to Atlanta on time. At exactly 11:00 p.m. the plane landed and went straight to our gate, arriving in the gate area at around 11:10. As we started to scurry to the train area, hoping and praying that our luggage arrived safely, there were lots of travelers coming in. I was surprised to see how busy the airport was at that time of night.

As we were going down the escalator to get to the train that would take us to baggage claim, I began to hear the all-too-familiar monotone, computerized voice blurt out over the terminal speakers, giving directions for the train schedule. It began, "This train is departing. The doors will close and *will not* reopen. Please step away from the doors." I looked at my husband and two girls as we were about to get off the escalator and said one word: "RUN!" So as fast as we could, we started dashing toward the first available train car.

As we were running and leaping, trying to get to a door that was obviously getting ready to close, I noticed something about the nearly packed train—no one was moving over or trying to make room for a family of four obviously giving it their best to get on *this* train. In fact, everyone was acting annoyed that we were even trying. Heaven forbid that we would have to wait another two minutes for the next train (smiles); however, we were bound and determined that we were going to make *this* train.

With everything in us we ran as fast as we could, and honestly, the doors were already beginning to close as the last one of us was coming on board. Jamie, the girls, and I were celebrating our small little accomplishment (feat, sprint, whatever you want to call it). We were high-fiving each other, saying, "Whew! Boy! Didn't think we would make that," when all of a sudden things seemed to start happening in slow motion. Out of nowhere a beautiful, young black girl came running frantically as fast as she possibly could, even faster than we were. *Was she trying to get on this train that we had just barely made? Was she really expecting to make it? Surely not!* But it was true; she was going for it. Astonished, we all (our family and the other passengers) watched this scenario take place right before our very eyes. This girl was seriously determined!

As she approached, the doors were literally closing, and she unbelievably jumped into the train and made it—with the exception of the coat she was wearing, which was caught in the train doors. That's when the monotone computer voice droned, "Something or someone is blocking the door. Please move away from the door."

Over and over this voice kept reverberating. I don't know who was louder, the computer voice or the voices of the people as they sighed and whispered disapprovingly. They were being just plain ol' rude. As she stood there, she suddenly said, "I'm stuck; I can't get through." But unfortunately agitation had set in for most of the people on that train, who were standing there in total disgust that this woman could not have waited just a few more minutes, including my husband. (Sorry, babe; I love you!)

As we stood there looking at this precarious situation, I said to my husband, "Would you please help her?" Now I was getting disgusted at his disgust. Although I have to admit, he is the one who had to drive us home, get the girls in bed—and then here is the hardest part—get them up before 7:00 a.m. and get them to school *on time*. This is something that my husband does so well (smiles!); I wouldn't dare take this anointing and bonding moment away from him by intruding!

Finally he got what was going on and summoned another gentleman, who was looking on with dismay, to help him. Together they stood on opposite sides of the woman to try and help her get unstuck. With one big heave they pulled her through the doors to freedom. *What happened next still runs chills up my spine.* As the young woman was released, she immediately fell into my arms and began to pour out her heart to me. "Oh, Judy Jacobs," she said, "I saw you coming down the escalator. I saw your black curly hair and your face as you were turning around and talking to your family on the escalator. And I thought, 'That's the woman of God. I've got to get to her.' Please pray for me. My family is torn apart, I am away from God, and I need help."

Right there in that underground train at Hartsfield-Jackson Atlanta International Airport, I began to lay hands on her and pray for her as the people in the train began to applaud. My husband, on the other hand, was giving her money, searching through his carry-on for CDs, DVDs, or something... it was really quite funny and very sobering all at the same time.

Now, what is the moral of that story? I will tell you. Someone is always watching you, especially if you name the name of Jesus. They want to see if all the things that you claim and proclaim are real. I mean, really for real! They want to see if you are "walking the walk" or just "talking the talk."

Real change has to come to our society, because we are the anointed ones God has chosen to change our culture. People look at us as "CHRIST-ians." The saying is true that we are the only Jesus most people will ever see. How are we going to reach these people in our nation and the people groups around the world, and especially our neighbors, if we, the church, don't show them Jesus? We must show them *who He is* through the genuine *power* of Almighty God, and that is His anointing, and especially His love. Jesus said, "All will know that you are My disciples, if you have love for one another" (John 13:35).

ARE YOU ZEALOUS FOR GOD AND HIS ANOINTING?

The Book of Romans is commonly considered the greatest exposition of Christian doctrine anywhere in Scripture. In this letter Paul took the time to expound on one of my favorite verses (which is also one of the most challenging verses) in the New Testament—Romans 12:11: "Do not lack diligence; be fervent in spirit; serve the Lord" (HCSB).

Bear with me on my new word, but this could possibly be one of the most "ginormous" yet smallest verses in the Bible. It gives us a clear picture of how God wants us to serve Him. This reminds me of Revelation 3:15–16, which says, "I know all the things you do, that you are neither hot nor cold. I wish that you were one or the other! But since you are like lukewarm water, neither hot nor cold, I will spit you out of my mouth!" (NLT).

In Romans 12 Paul was admonishing us to be and do three things: to be diligent, to be fervent, and to serve.

The word *diligence* comes from the Greek term *spoudē* (pronounced spoo-day'), which means "speed...dispatch, eagerness, earnestness."[3] The wording for Romans 12:11 in the New International Version reads, "Never be lacking in zeal, but keep your spiritual fervor, serving the Lord."

Perhaps the best thing ever written about Christian zeal comes from Bishop J. C. Ryle of Liverpool, England. In the 1800s he preached a sermon titled "Be Zealous," stating that the subject of zeal cannot be passed over by any serious student of the Word:

> Zeal in religion [or *relationship*] is a burning desire to please God, to do His will, and to advance His glory in the world in every possible way. It is a desire which no man feels by nature,—which the Spirit puts in the heart of every believer when he is converted,—but which some believers feel so much more strongly than other ones, that they alone deserve to be called zealous men.
>
> This desire is so strong, when it really reigns in a man, that it impels him to make any sacrifice,—to go through any trouble,—to deny himself to any amount,—to suffer, to work, to labour, to toil,—to spend himself and be spent, and even to die,—if only they can please God and honour Christ.
>
> ...He only sees one thing,—he cares for one thing,—he lives for one thing,—he is swallowed up in one thing, and that *one thing* is to please God. Whether he lives, or whether he dies,—whether he has health, or whether he has sickness,—whether he is rich, or whether he is poor,—whether he pleases man, or whether he gives offence,—whether he is thought wise, or whether he is thought foolish,—whether he gets blame, or whether he gets praise,—whether he gets

honour, or whether he gets shame,—for all this the zealous man cares nothing at all. *He burns for one thing*; and that one thing is to please God, and to advance God's glory.[4]

The Bible gives an account of the prophet Elijah being taken up to heaven in a fiery chariot. Before he was taken, "Elijah said to Elisha, 'Ask! What may I do for you, before I am taken away from you?' Elisha said, 'Please let a double portion of your spirit be upon me.' So he said, 'You have asked a hard thing. Nevertheless, if you see me when I am taken from you, it shall be so for you; but if not, it shall not be so'" (2 Kings 2:9–10).

When the horses and chariots of fire came down to pick up Elijah, *Elisha saw it,* and immediately the mantle (i.e., the prayer shawl or tallit) fell upon him (v. 13). Elisha got exactly what he asked for. He received a mantle not only in the natural but also in the supernatural. From then on, everywhere he went everyone identified with him because people related to him as having been with Elijah, since he had Elijah's mantle (2 Kings 3:11).

I want you to know that if you are seeking hard after God and are searching diligently to thrive in His anointing, a mantle already rests upon you to change your culture and society. Everywhere you go, you are carrying the mantle of Jesus Christ, who ascended to heaven and has called you to pick up His anointing. You carry it to the grocery store, the bank, and the office, and through prayer you can literally carry it around the world.

Someone is hurting, crying, and longing for the truth. Someone is seeking redemption and freedom from fears, pain, and heartache. People are looking for real answers to the dilemmas they face, and sometimes they will let someone in who just looks like they have the answer. *But the truth of the matter is this: we know the One who can save, deliver, and set them free. His name is JESUS.*

Faith Works Through Love

How can we change our society and culture? Jesus said, "You are not of the world" (John 15:19). Absolutely! And we are not supposed to be! According to Jesus, we are "the light of the world. A city that is set on a hill" that can't be hidden. We are the "salt of the earth" that makes people thirsty. (See Matthew 5:13–14.) One of the best ways that we can be "salt" and "light" is to love like Jesus loved. Here are a few inspiring examples.

I love Jeannie, who is one of our mentees. She is an incredible woman who lives in the inner city of Fort Myers, Florida. Her passion is to reach pole dancers and their children. She has hair that is spiked and dyed purple, and she loves to go into these places. During the dancers' breaks she goes in and takes them gift baskets, toiletries, little gifts for their children, and stuff to just get them through the month. Many of these women feel trapped and hopeless until Jeannie shows up with hope, spreads God's love, and stimulates faith in them that they can have a better life. Many of them have come off the poles and gotten saved and baptized. They have earned their GEDs, acquired a skill, and are leading joyful, normal lives. People like Jeannie are changing their culture and society with the love of God.

Here's a story about a man named William Booth, who started small and built a powerful work for God.

> In 1865, William Booth, an ordained Methodist minister, aided by his wife Catherine, formed an evangelical group dedicated to preaching among the unchurched people living in the midst of terrible poverty in London's East End.
>
> Booth's ministry recognized the interdependence of material, emotional, and spiritual needs. In addition to preaching the gospel of Jesus Christ, Booth became involved

in the feeding and shelter of the hungry and homeless and in rehabilitation of alcoholics.

William Booth's congregation was desperately poor. He preached hope and salvation....

In 1867, Booth had only 10 full-time workers. By 1874, the numbers had grown to 1,000 volunteers and 42 evangelists.[5]

Now, The Salvation Army is active in virtually every corner of the world.

In this new century, The Salvation Army is serving more people in the USA than ever before. We are already seeing large increases in the number of Americans seeking the basic necessities of life—food, shelter, and warmth. Approximately 30 million people received help from The Salvation Army in 2011, but the magnitude of the mission facing The Salvation Army in communities throughout the United States remains great.[6]

What started out as a man and a woman wanting to see people's lives changed by the power of Jesus Christ developed into a world of love and care for people in over 106 nations, with 3.5 million volunteers.[7] *God is always looking for someone who will be the change agent to bring the change!*

Apostle Shirley Arnold has been taking groups into India for many years to evangelize. Years ago, while she and her team were in the "red light district" witnessing and telling people about the love of Christ, she happened upon a beautiful lady, not knowing at the time that not only was she a prostitute but she was also a "madam," which means she had many young ladies under her who answered to her whom she was accountable for. And she was in serious bondage because she had to answer to her pimp.

The team kept going back to the same place and the same lady every time they went back to this part of India. After much prayer and perseverance it finally paid off. The madam got saved, and, you guessed it, she led her entire brothel to Jesus! They all came off the streets, were baptized, and were discipled. Today these same ladies are bringing women off the streets to a saving knowledge of Jesus Christ. They are all in a picture on my prayer wall, and every time I see their beautiful faces it makes me cry to see just how good God is.

We can do it! We can take up the mantle of the Lord and bring salvation, healing, and deliverance to a dying world: not in our own strength but by the anointing of God that resides in us. *I say to you now: someone is waiting for you to come right where they are, in the midst of their "hell," and touch them with the love of Jesus.*

Another International Institute of Mentoring mentee posted a very thought-provoking story. It relates to how we handle pressure, if we are affected by things in life or if we actually *affect our environment and bring change.* Enjoy this with me. It is titled "Carrots, Eggs, or Coffee: Which One Are You?"[8]

> A young woman went to her grandmother and told her about her life and how things were so hard for her. She did not know how she was going to make it and wanted to give up. She was tired of fighting and struggling. It seemed as one problem was solved a new one arose.
>
> Her grandmother took her to the kitchen. She filled three pots with water. In the first, she placed carrots; in the second, she placed eggs; and in the last, she placed ground coffee beans. She let them sit and boil without saying a word.
>
> In about twenty minutes she turned off the burners. She fished the carrots out and placed them in a bowl. She pulled the eggs out and placed them in a bowl. Then she ladled [poured] the coffee out and placed it in a bowl. Turning to her granddaughter, she asked, "Tell me, what do you see?"

"Carrots, eggs, and coffee," she replied.

She brought her closer and asked her to feel the carrots. She did and noted that they got soft. She then asked her to take an egg and break it.

After pulling off the shell, she observed the hard-boiled egg.

Finally, she asked her to sip the coffee. The granddaughter smiled as she tasted its rich aroma. The granddaughter then asked, "What's the point, Grandmother?"

Her grandmother explained that each of these objects had faced the same adversity—boiling water—but each reacted differently.

The carrot went in strong, hard, and unrelenting. However, after being subjected to the boiling water, it softened and became weak. The egg had been fragile. Its thin outer shell had protected its liquid interior. But after sitting through the boiling water, its inside became hardened.

The ground coffee beans were unique, however. After they were in the boiling water, they had changed the water.

"Which are you?" she asked her granddaughter. "When adversity knocks on your door, how do you respond? Are you a carrot, an egg, or a coffee bean?"

Think of this: Which am I? Am I the carrot that seems strong, but with pain and adversity, do I wilt and become soft and lose my strength? Am I the egg that starts with a malleable heart, but changes with the heat? Did I have a fluid spirit, but after a death, a breakup, a financial hardship or some other trial, have I become hardened and stiff? Does my shell look the same, but on the inside am I bitter and tough with a stiff spirit and a hardened heart?

Or am I like the coffee bean? The bean actually changes the hot water, the very circumstance that brings the pain. When the water gets hot, it releases the fragrance and flavor.

If you are like the bean, when things are at their worst,

you get better and change the situation around you. When the hours are the darkest and trials are their greatest, do you elevate to another level?

—Author Unknown

When I think of this story, it reminds me of 2 Corinthians 12:10, which declares, "When I am weak, then I am strong." I'll say it again: we are created to come before God in true worship and change the atmosphere around us. You can do it! You are anointed for this!

Always remember, our challenges are never about us. Someone else is always hurting worse than we are—possibly someone we know, someone who needs more than we could ever imagine. We must be the ones to change this society and culture…and it always starts with the person who is right in front of us, the one who is closest to us.

When I think of this next story, I remember the words of J. Hudson Taylor, who said: "The Great Commission is not an option to be considered, but a command to be obeyed."[9] Read this story with me.

It's All About John 3:16

The story is told of a young man in an upper Northern city who had lost his parents in a car accident and was left to fend for himself. The young man would go out every day and try to sell newspapers to help get food to eat.

One particular cold day, with several feet of snow on the ground, he was out as usual, trying to sell his newspapers. Because of the cold weather, he wasn't selling many papers. He walked up to a policeman and asked, "Mister, you don't know where a poor boy could find a warm place to sleep tonight, do you? I sleep in a box around the corner and down the alley, and it's awful cold in there at night. It sure would be nice to have a warm place to stay."

The policeman looked down at the boy and told him, "Go down

the street to the big white house and knock on the door. When they open the door, just tell them 'John 3:16' and they will let you in."

This seemed very strange and weird to the young boy, but nevertheless, there was something in the policeman's eyes that he felt he could trust, so he promised him that he would do it, and then off he went.

He walked down the street until he came to the big white house. Hesitantly he walked up to the door and got up enough nerve to ring the doorbell. After a very brief moment, sure enough, this very nice elderly lady came to the door and said, "Yes, may I help you?"

The young man just followed the instructions he had been given and very softly and gingerly said, "John 3:16." Immediately the woman's expression changed. She said to the him, "Oh, my goodness, come on in, come on in; it is so cold outside. Come over and warm yourself by the nice fireplace, and I'll be right back."

He was mesmerized by what had just happened. He very quickly went over to the blazing fireplace that felt so incredibly great. He couldn't remember the last time he was that warm and unthawed. He thought to himself, "John 3:16...I don't understand it, but it sure makes a boy feel warm."

In just a few short minutes, it seemed, the lady came back and took him into this lovely dining room where a gigantic bowl of hot chicken soup was waiting, along with some hot, fresh bread. The lady said, "Eat as much as you like; there is plenty more where that came from." The boy ate and ate, until he couldn't eat another bite. Again he thought, "John 3:16...I still don't understand, but it surely makes a hungry boy feel full."

The night was pressing in, and the lady took him upstairs to a huge bathtub filled with warm water. As he soaked in that warm, sudsy water, he thought, "John 3:16...even though I don't understand it, it sure makes a dirty boy feel clean."

When he had finished and had nightclothes on, the lady came

and got him. She took him into a bedroom and tucked him into a big feather bed, pulling the covers up to his neck and kissing him goodnight. As he lay there in the darkness, falling off to sleep, he thought, "John 3:16...I don't understand it yet, but it sure makes a tired boy feel rested."

The next morning when he awakened, the lady came and took him back to the dining table filled with food. After he had eaten, she sat down next to him, with a Bible in her hand, and asked him, "Do you understand John 3:16?"

"No, ma'am," he answered. "The first time I ever heard it was last night when the policeman told me to say 'John 3:16.'"

She opened the Bible to John 3:16 and explained to him about Jesus. Right there he gave his life to Jesus, thinking, "John 3:16...I don't understand it completely, but it sure makes a lost boy feel safe."[10]

Don't be deceived, misconceived, or swayed; the anointing is still about John 3:16: *"For God so loved the world that He gave His only begotten Son, that whoever believes in Him should not perish but have everlasting life"* (emphasis added). We have the ability and the capacity through the power of the Holy Spirit to change people's lives, and in the meantime, God can absolutely change our society and our culture through a yielded vessel. That vessel is you!

⟳ LET IT BE to ME...

Have you ever considered that you have been anointed with the love and generosity of Almighty God? Oh, yes, you have! It happened when you first believed in Jesus Christ, when you first experienced His love and kindness. Knowing God and walking in the anointing is all about John 3:16. The love that is inside of you is so powerful it can change the very society and culture you live in—starting with the people closest to you. You—*yes, you*—are anointed to show your love for God by freely and consistently giving His love to others.

Now, when you think about the stories in this chapter, how have you embraced this holy calling and purpose for your life? Have you been "walking the walk," taking advantage of every opportunity to share His love, or have you more often just been "talking the talk," too busy or too tired to pause and help someone in need? Are you a carrot, an egg, or a coffee bean when it comes to handling the stress and pressures of life? Are you, by the power of the anointing, changing the atmosphere around you?

Whatever your response may be, I pray that for the rest of your days the zeal of the Lord will ignite a holy passion in you, a passion that burns so hot that you wake up every day on fire to live out God's mission…even if nobody else is looking. I pray this, my friend, because you have been anointed for such a time as this!

ten

THE MENTORING ANOINTING

For I long to see you, that I may impart to you some spiritual gift,
so that you may be established—that is, that I may be encour-
aged together with you by the mutual faith both of you and me.

—ROMANS 1:11–12

FROM EVERYTHING YOU have read, meditated about, declared, and worked through up to this point, it is more than obvious: because you belong to Jesus Christ, you are anointed! And as you have picked up throughout this book, especially in chapter 9, God wants you to impact others through the power of His anointing. *That means, like Paul, whose words appear above, you are called to be a mentor.* And I have good news: you already possess the most powerful mentoring anointing there is—because the master mentor, Jesus Christ, lives in you.

So let's look deeper into the name that is above every name. Now, you need to understand that "Christ" was not Jesus's last name (smiles). The name *Jesus* comes from the Greek word *Iēsous* (pronounced ee-ay-sooce'), which is transliterated from the Hebrew and means, "Jehovah is salvation."[1] In Greek the name *Christ* comes from the word *Christos* (pronounced khris-tos'), which means, "anointed; i.e., the Messiah."[2] In essence, when we say the name *Jesus Christ,* we are proclaiming, "Salvation Anointed Messiah." I love the sound of these words! Through Jesus's anointing we are so much more than we could ever be without Him.

Bishop Harry R. Jackson, pastor of Hope Christian Church in Beltsville, Maryland, shares this wonderful revelation about the anointing Jesus has extended to us:

> The anointing is the empowerment of God that allows us to exceed our natural abilities and leaves lasting fruit that honors Jesus Christ. This primarily is received by faith and operates in a unique realm of grace. It gives glory to God in several ways. First of all, it is part of the witness of Christ's reality in the earth. It is what Paul refers to in 1 Corinthians 1:27, that God chose the foolish things to shame the wise. Second, the anointing is also one of several things Paul speaks about in 1 Corinthians 1:30–31, when he says, "You are in Christ Jesus, who became for us wisdom from God—and righteousness and sanctification and redemption—that... 'He who glories, let him glory in the LORD.'"[3]

Amen! Because of what Christ has done, there is nothing else we can do but boast in the Lord. "Salvation Anointed Messiah" has done it all... He became the wisdom of God for us and has freely given us righteousness, sanctification, and redemption. He finished His work on Calvary, and because He is the greatest mentor the world has ever known, *Jesus made sure His work would continue* by sending us the Holy Spirit, the "Spirit of truth," the Comforter who lives in us. Just as Jesus promised, the Holy Spirit guides us into all truth, teaches us all things, and tells us things that are to come. (See John 14:17; 16:7–15.)

Yes, when Jesus died on the cross *once for all,* He made sure *all* who received Him would have the help they need, every day of their lives, for the rest of their lives. He set the plan in motion shortly after telling the disciples in Acts 1:8, "But you shall receive power when the Holy Spirit has come upon you; and you shall be witnesses to Me…" After declaring the Father's plan, Jesus ascended to heaven (v. 9). Why? It was time for the disciples (His mentees) to take it from there. *That's what I call anointed mentorship!* I say to you: the proof of the perfect mentorship of Jesus Christ is the "mentoring anointing" that flows from the Holy Spirit through you and me.

WHO, ME? A MENTOR?

What I love about the anointing is that it is *portable.* Jesus, the Anointed One, changed the atmosphere everywhere He went throughout His ministry: mentoring the disciples, teaching, preaching, praying, and doing signs, wonders, and miracles. That means you can take the anointing with you wherever you go. If you carry Jesus with you (and you do!), you carry His anointing with you also.

First John 2:27 declares: "The anointing you received from God remains in you, and you do not need anyone to teach you this. Instead, because God's anointing teaches you about everything and is true and not a lie, abide in him, as he taught you to do" (ISV). The "anointing" in this verse speaks of the Holy Spirit.

Unfortunately there are a lot of people who want to be mentored, but when it comes down to it, they don't want anyone telling them to step out of their comfort zone. Then there are those who need to be pouring out their hearts, lives, and experiences into someone else, but they find themselves being concerned for their "four and no more."

I heard Bishop Jakes give a definition of the word *mentoring,* and I have never forgotten it. He said it was, "Men-touring-your-life." Did you get that? Like I said before, if you claim the name of Jesus, someone is always watching you. Somebody, somewhere is touring and watching your every move. My husband often reminds the godly fathers in our church that they have a church too. It is called their family. David said, "I will lead a life of integrity in my own home" (Ps. 101:2, NLT). That's where it all begins, my friend, right there in your own home.

Paul said in 1 Corinthians 11:1, "Be ye followers of me, even as I also am of Christ" (KJV). Paul gave the instruction and the prerequisite in the same sentence. If the leadership you are under starts to "go south" and they are not following the Word of God (which is our final authority), don't just walk out of there—*run!* Now I'm not necessarily talking about family members. If a family member—a husband, son, daughter, or anyone you love—falls into error, there is that really bad word that you have to do to make it: *work!* Yuck! What a nasty word. Nobody likes to work.

The Book of Hebrews records:

> You have been believers so long now that you ought to be teaching others. Instead, you need someone to teach you again the basic things about God's word [or about the oracles of God]. You are like babies who need milk and cannot eat solid food. For someone who lives on milk is still an infant and doesn't know how to do what is right. Solid food is for those who are mature, who through training have the skill to recognize the difference between right and wrong.
> —HEBREWS 5:12–14, NLT

If you are living a life of true worship to the Lord, you know the difference between right and wrong. You just need to believe God, step up to the call, and submit to the mentoring anointing. Let it flow through you to others. Communicate, reason, pray, read the Word...do what the Anointed One leads you to do so someone else can come up higher and begin to flow in God's purpose for their lives. And here is another one: somebody has to be *mature!* It might as well be you. Amen!

God declared in Psalm 101:6, "I will search for faithful people to be my companions" (NLT). Mentoring involves a lot of work. It takes people who are resolved to the fact that they have a purpose in God. These are people who have a made-up mind that declares: "I am going to do everything I possibly can to see God be the 'all in all' in me." So what are you waiting for? *It's time!* Get up off of your knees, roll up your sleeves, and go to work! I declare you will prosper in this anointing as you believe God and take the first step of faith.

A Diamond in the Rough

She came from Blantyre, Malawi, in Central Africa. Her name is Martha Nantoka. Martha had seen us ministering on a webcast from World Harvest Church, where Pastor Rod Parsley serves as the senior pastor, in Columbus, Ohio. We were there as guests for his Dominion Camp Meeting in 2004.

I was asked to bring the Word for an afternoon service. There was a great crowd, and I was excited to have the distinct honor of ministering at this amazing conference. But just before I did, I proceeded to promote and invite people to our International Institute of Mentoring (IIOM) that would be coming up soon. You see, the IIOM (as I will refer to it) is one of my most fervent passions. I love to sing and minister through the preached Word of God every chance I get. (If you know me at all, you know I love to sing.) I have been singing since I was old enough to talk. Also, unlike a lot of people I know, I truly enjoy doing television and reaching masses of people. But if you want to talk about what my *real passion* is, then it would have to be *mentoring.*

And that's how I met Martha. As I was explaining onstage what the IIOM was, its vision and what it represented, I had Martha's attention. As she watched by webcast, she became more and more interested, so much so that she got all the information and immediately contacted us shortly after we returned home from the conference.

She had been extremely interested in trying to locate a mentor for a long while. At the time, she was pastoring a thriving church in Malawi while her husband, Roy, ws in the United States working on his doctoral degree in theology. *There was only one problem: Martha felt less than adequate to pastor a church.* After much prayer she felt that she desperately needed a mentor, and so she started to pray and fast and seek the Lord as to what she should do.

As God would have it, Martha felt within her heart that getting involved in the IIOM is what she should pursue. With her husband's blessing she inquired, and when she contacted our office, she had no money and no means of coming, but she had a real hunger to learn and to be teachable. My husband and I and the IIOM mentors agreed that we should pay her airfare and take care of her expenses while she was in our city for five days. We wanted to make an investment in this beautiful servant of Christ.

When she arrived, she was so shy that she wouldn't look anyone in the eyes. She bowed her head and was constantly bowing in front of me, no matter how many times I told her, "Martha, you don't have to bow in front of me. Martha, look me in the eyes." I know a lot of this had to do with her culture, and she was truly grateful for the opportunity. She wanted to show her gratitude, but we needed to get this mighty woman of God *believing* that she *truly was* a mighty woman of God and that she was *anointed.*

As we began to impart into Martha, along with the other dynamic speakers whom we had assembled for these sessions, I made sure I kept her very close. God had His hand upon her, and I could see it. *A mentor sees what you can't see and hears what you can't hear.* What did I see in the natural? I saw a brown, skinny, round-faced woman with desperation in her eyes for the supernatural. Her shoulders drooped, her back was bent, and her head was down—but there was more to this lady, and I knew it.

What did I see in the Spirit and in the anointing? I saw a massive giant of a woman, with a face set like flint, shoulders back, head up, eyes piercing with the power of God! I saw a devil-stomping, demon-busting, anointed vessel of the living Jehovah God. I saw a "diamond in the rough," a vessel that was as "bold as a lion."

Let me explain. I saw all of this in the Spirit, and believe me when I tell you, it wasn't there in the natural. What I love about God is that He sees all of us like that. If He were to judge me by what others saw in me, or even by what I was able to see in myself, you would have never even heard of me, much less be reading this book. *But look at God!* He doesn't judge us by man's standards but by His own standards. Man looks at the outside, but God looks at the heart (1 Sam. 16:7).

The Bible declares in 1 Samuel 10:6 that Samuel told Saul, "Then the Spirit of the LORD will come upon you, and you will prophesy with them [a group of prophets] and be turned into another man." This is exactly what happened to Martha. The more she came to the IIOM, the more God began to do such an incredible work in her life and in the lives of others around her.

Later she and her husband decided to bring their family to the States to keep the family together and intact. So she moved up North and continued to attend the IIOM Main Events and Intensives throughout the year. I remember one event in particular when our special guest was *Charisma* magazine's former editor Lee Grady. It was a powerful night as Lee ministered on the Great Commission. When he got to the end of his message, the Holy Spirit began to move mightily upon the people. Lee received the word of the Lord and began to declare it. He prophesied there was someone in the room whom God was going to use mightily in Africa, and then he gave an invitation and instructed anyone who felt the call to go to Africa to come forward.

Several people came forward for prayer, and Martha was one of them, responding to the call upon her life. As Lee Grady began to pray for all of those who felt the call to Africa, he got to Martha and began to pray for her. Suddenly she was overwhelmed by the

Spirit of God and was slain, and I do mean slain, in the Spirit. So much so that hours later after the service had ended and everyone was almost gone from the building, she was still lying there on the floor with the Spirit of God shooting throughout her body. Several people had to literally get her up off the floor. They managed to pick her up, get her in the car, and then safely lay her down so they could get her back to her room. She woke up the next day with some incredible things to say.

Martha testified to the fact that she had an encounter with God and that it was the encounter of her life. She spoke of seeing a vision of her going from village to village showing *The Passion of the Christ* movie. She said that God had told her if she would obey, He would give her many nations in Africa. Martha was so excited to get home and share the vision with her husband. Likewise he was excited when she shared the amazing vision from God, and they set out immediately to arrange an appointment with their presiding bishop.

The day finally came for them to share this incredible vision with someone whom they believed would release them with a blessing to go and do the work of the Lord. What they actually encountered was the exact opposite. Their bishop told them, "Let me pray about it for three days; come back, and I will tell you what God said." Three days passed, and they came back to his office. He cut right to the chase. "I'm sorry, Sister Martha, I can't release you to go back to Africa to do the things you are requesting because you are a woman, and I cannot release you to go." Martha and Pastor Roy sat there at first, stunned and in disbelief. Then the authority and boldness of God came over Sister Martha.

With as much respect as she could muster up, she told the bishop, "With all due respect, sir, my husband has released me and God is the one who has placed this in my heart. One day I will have to give an account to Him, so I must obey God rather than man."

With that, they left his office and have not looked back since. That was six years ago, and to date she has seen almost a million people come to Jesus. She has also helped to establish legislation that no child can be sold to older men for their enjoyment. If caught, they will spend at least fifty years in prison. Now beautiful young children and young women have been rescued because of the anointing on this one woman's life. What can be done in obedience to the unction of the Holy Spirit still remains to be seen. God is looking for people who are *willing* and *obedient*.

MENTORING = DISCIPLESHIP

As mentors and coaches in the day and age that we are living in, we have to see beyond our own comforts and luxuries. We still have a lost world to win, and if we set out to fulfill our purpose, we are going to have to train and mentor a large army. We need to get them prepared and ready for what lies ahead very quickly. It will take every believer, trusting God right where they are and reaching out to others, to fulfill the mentoring anointing. The apostle John wrote:

> I write unto you, little children, because your sins are forgiven you for his name's sake. I write unto you, fathers, because ye have known him that is *from the beginning*. ["You have known him *who has always existed*" (PHILLIPS).]...I have written unto you, young men, because ye are *strong* ["because you are strong and *vigorous*" (AMP)], and the word of God *abideth* in you ["you have a *hold on God's truth*" (PHILLIPS)], and ye have *overcome* the wicked one ["*mastered*" (NEB); "*conquered*" (NET)].
>
> —1 JOHN 2:12–14, KJV, EMPHASIS ADDED

A commentary from the *New Spirit-Filled Life Bible*, edited by Jack Hayford, gives us more insight into this process and why God has called and anointed every believer to become a mentor:

When a baby is born biologically, he has everything he needs for adulthood. He just has to grow into it. The same is true with our spiritual progress. Godly growth is a providential journey of becoming what we already are. These two verses do not refer to ages as much as stages of godly development. As infants or "little children," we are excited about the newness of our relationship with God. But as we feed on the milk of the word (1 Pet. 2:2), we learn that there is more to salvation than the forgiveness of our sins. We grow beyond our infancy into young adult lives of challenge and victory as people who live daily by faith (2 Cor. 5:7). Finally, "fatherhood" is that designation given to saints who have come to know God as friend. Fathers know the joy and peace of intimacy with the Lord and endeavor to begin producing spiritual offspring through the loving process of discipleship. (Matt. 28:19, 20).[4]

True Mentorship ... Seeing Each Other Through

Sometimes we get so caught up in religious terms and stiff, formal systems that we forget mentoring is just a normal process of everyday life. *God makes it simple: as He grows us, we help others to grow.* Parents learn this as we raise our children, workers apply this as they move up the corporate ladder, and as believers, we must always be mindful that while we are *looking up* and *moving up* in the things of God, we must *keep reaching back* to give someone a helping hand. One thing is sure: we all *get what we need* and *get where we're going* when we do things together.

It is a privilege when God trusts us with what He treasures most: *people*. He loves people so deeply that He teaches us what we need to know so that at the right moment we can help somebody in need. Isaiah 50:4 states, "The Sovereign Lord has given me an instructed tongue, to know the word that sustains the weary. He wakens me morning by morning, wakens my ear to listen like one being taught" (NIV).

It has been my privilege and honor to be able to mentor hundreds of God's people coming through the IIOM. I have not done this by myself. No one ever does anything worthwhile by themselves. Jamie and I have had some very strong and powerful men and women—professionals, stay-at-home moms, and just people who love people—help us to see lives changed, visions stretched, and ministry goals reached. This continues to be my greatest passion.

I love this anonymous saying: *God has not called us to see through each other, but to see each other through.* Oh, yes! That is what true mentoring is all about: helping to see people through things that are either holding them down, holding them back, or holding them up.

Some of the people God has called you to mentor live right in your own home: that son or daughter, niece or nephew, or other family member. There are also others you see on a regular basis: a friend at work, a child or teenager at church, a young mother, a young married couple…the list could go on and on. *Whom does God want you to pour yourself into?* The enemy of our souls wants us to think we are not effective in reaching our own children and the people we love most, but as we know, he is a liar. The following story is evidence of this fact.

> One mother affected her child's life in ways that, in turn, impacted millions of people in the United States. The child's father was an abusive alcoholic, yet in spite of this, his mother constantly repeated a simple phrase over and over again to her son. She would say, "God has a plan for your life. There is purpose and worth to each and every life." This man grew up to be a man "whose soul could be heard in his voice," a man with a personal life goal of "cheering up those he met." And as I recently watched this man's funeral on TV, I was captivated in considering the impact

of his mother's vision for a noble life purpose. An inscription on the front of the library that was built in his honor reads, "There is purpose and worth to each and every life." President Ronald Reagan's mother planted the seeds of noble purpose in his life.

As a young boy, Ronald Reagan moved all over the US because of his father's abusive life-style. However, his mother's steady message of hope influenced him more deeply than his abusive father wounded him.[5]

I read a John Maxwell quote that is so powerful that I want my children, my church family, and especially my IIOM family to know it. He said, "I want to make a difference with people making a difference, doing something that makes a difference at a time when it makes a difference."[6]

We are the ones who make a difference in our culture and society. *What legacy will we leave? Who will follow us? What kind of trail and testimony are we leaving behind?* The Bible tells us that without a vision, people perish (Prov. 29:18, KJV). Someone has said, "A dream is something you see with your eyes closed. A vision is something you see with your eyes open." Come on; open up those eyes and get someone to come alongside of you and see it with you! Better yet, *you* become the "seer of the vision" for somebody else, and then help them to accomplish it—all for His glory.

You Can Become FAT in the Mentoring Anointing!

Finally, I encourage you to be a "FAT" Christian. "What is that?", you might ask. I know what you're thinking, and it's not *that* (smiles). I am speaking of an acronym:

F—Faithful

A—Available

T—Teachable

- Be faithful to the call that He has placed on your life. David said, "Lord, where are the faithful people? Those who stick with something and do it with excellence and do it right the first time. The people you can depend on. Where are they? They are disappearing on the earth" (Ps. 12:1, author's paraphrase).

- Be available. Isaiah heard the Lord say, "Who will go for Us?" His response was, "Here am I! Send me" (Isa. 6:8). God always uses available people, and oftentimes they are going to be busy people. Doctors, lawyers, tax collectors, fishermen…all of them were busy people. God is looking for someone who will just say that simple word *yes*.

- Be teachable. As we know, in order for a child to become a successful adult, he or she must constantly be in a learning process, being mentored by parents and family, teachers, preachers, and life. We must be teachable because God can't teach anything to a know-it-all. One thing you will always be doing until Jesus comes back is learning. I never get to the point where I feel like I know it all. When Jesus wanted to show some people what the kingdom of heaven looked like, He showed them a child. Then He said, "Whoever does not receive the kingdom of God as a little child will by no means enter it" (Luke 18:17).

The mentoring anointing is upon you—not only to become a mentor but also to be mentored yourself. Either way, you must be

"FAT" to thrive in this anointing. So, come on; eat up the Word of God and obediently follow the leading of the Holy Spirit! You are called to be a mentor.

∞ LET IT BE to ME . . .

Jesus Christ, "Salvation Anointed Messiah," is the *master mentor* who set everything in place for you to walk in His anointing. In Him, because of His finished work, you can become all you dream and more. But don't make the mistake of **looking up** and *moving up* without *reaching back*. This violates the very principle that has brought you this far in your walk with God.

Now let me ask: Are you seasoned in the things of God, or are you a "diamond in the rough"? Could you use a little help to go farther in your kingdom purpose? Do you see weak areas in others that are either holding them down, back, or up? Remember, "God has not called us to see through each other, but to see each other through." Go back and take another look at Martha's story. *What things did she do as she flowed in the mentoring anointing that you may need to do right now?*

Take a few moments to do this little prayer exercise—and have your journal handy: (1) Ask the Lord to expose areas in your life that could be improved with anointed mentorship. (2) Ask Him to open your eyes to the people He wants you to mentor. Write everything He reveals to you in your journal and stay open throughout the day, every day, for more direction.

I thank God for helping you to be **F**aithful, **A**vailable, and **T**eachable, because you already possess the most powerful mentorship anointing ever known to man. You just have to grow into it, *and grow into it you will*—because you are anointed for this!

eleven

THE ANOINTING *to* PROSPER

And God is able to make all grace abound toward
you, that you, always having all sufficiency in all things,
may have an abundance for every good work.

—2 Corinthians 9:8

G
OD HONORS FAITHFULNESS and humility, and He is constantly looking for ways to bless you. Sometimes He will use the most unlikely and unusual situations to bless you. You just have to keep your eyes wide open to what God has for you. God wants to use somebody to show Himself strong through, and I believe you are anointed for this! You are anointed to prosper during this time and season in your life.

It is God's will for you to prosper and be in health, even as you are enjoying being a joyful Christian who loves God. The anointing to prosper is in you. I have never met a soul who says, "I have too much money," or, "I just love being poor and hungry, cold and destitute. I just love doing without." Never! Every person I meet loves to have enough, and then some left over. Everybody enjoys driving a nice car. Every woman I know loves the idea of having her own home. God put it in us to prosper. How did He do it? Consider this verse:

> But it was the LORD's good plan to crush him [Jesus] and
> cause him grief. Yet when his life is made an offering for
> sin, he will have many descendants. He will enjoy a long
> life, and the LORD's good plan will prosper in his hands.
>
> —ISAIAH 53:10, NLT

Did you get that? Because Jesus suffered and became the final
offering for sin, God's plan always *prospers* in His hands. And we
are His descendants! That means that as we walk in God's plan and
purpose, we can be confident that it is His will for us to prosper.
As we remain humbly obedient to God, He will cause all grace to
abound toward us so we have sufficiency in all things and an abun-
dant supply for every good work.

I love the words of Winston Churchill, who once said, "What is
the use in living, if it be not to strive for noble causes and to make
this muddled world a better place for those who will live in it after
we are gone?"[1] *I say to you: the Lord wants you to prosper and be
in health, even as your soul prospers!* When you walk in the purpose of God, freely giving, helping others, and changing the atmosphere around you for His glory, God releases *His life* through you.
And He builds a new life for you: a life that is greater than you
could have built on your own. I tell you: God is faithful. He blesses
you for your obedience.

GOD PROSPERS YOU FOR A PURPOSE

In her book *The Carr Guide to Personal Wealth*, Dr. Deena Carr
observes:

> It is clear that we are living in very challenging times of great
> change—some of the most momentous for the U.S. and
> globally. In the midst of this, however, there is significant
> opportunity for great financial success, but there is also the
> risk of devastating financial collapse.[2]

She goes on to say, and I paraphrase: "The seed is a powerful and popular concept in the Bible. It traditionally refers to a number of things, including: the harvest of grain, fruit, etc.; lineage or children; the Word of God; the kingdom of heaven; and faith. Financial security comes as a result of a process that is always grounded first and foremost in God. We do not have to wait for 'luck' or a 'winning lottery ticket.' The Creator has placed in His children the ability to access His abundance."[3]

Then Dr. Carr confirms:

> Over the past twenty years, my work with major financial institutions has reaffirmed my belief that faith and finances work hand in hand. It has affirmed for me that God is the creator of all things, including wealth. He is not broke, and we shouldn't be either.[4]

The Bible declares, "And you shall remember the LORD your God, for it is He who gives you the power [the Holy Spirit–empowered ability and anointing] to get wealth, that He may establish His covenant" (Deut. 8:18). In the same thought process Hebrews 7:7 declares, "And without question, the person who has the power to give a blessing is greater than the one who is blessed" (NLT). That means if God has blessed me to bless you, then it is a greater blessing for me to bless you than it is for me to receive a blessing. This is why the Bible says, "It is more blessed to give than to receive" (Acts 20:35).

Notice when Jesus said, "Give," He also said, "And it will be given unto you." What you need to grasp when you're giving to God is this: giving and receiving go hand in hand. They belong together. Only when we give are we in a position to expect to receive a harvest. I love the interest rate that Jesus describes when you give: "…good measure, pressed down, shaken together, and running over" (Luke 6:38).

My husband and I do not love anything better than being able to give to our daughters. It is such a joy and delight to see their countenance change when we bring them something home from a trip or take them to their favorite store in the mall to let them pick something out just to bless them. This works the same way with the Father. Jesus said in Luke 12:32, "Do not fear, little flock, for it is your Father's good pleasure to give you the kingdom." I don't care what you have heard or what type of negativity has been crammed down your throat; it is *not* God's will for you to be in lack, poverty, sickness, and disease. It is *not* His will for you to go through life broke, busted, and disgusted.

David said in Psalm 35:27, "Let the LORD be magnified, who has *pleasure* in the prosperity of His servant" (emphasis added).

Let me ask you: Are you His servant? Are you His child? Then according to His Word, God takes *great pleasure* in *your prosperity.* Do you know why? So that His will may be established in the earth. And what is His will? Let's remember chapter 9 and John 3:16. *God is not willing for anyone to perish.* This is the very heartbeat of the Father. He is all about *souls!* That's why He wants you to be anointed to prosper.

Jesus declared, "And this gospel of the kingdom will be preached in all the world as a witness to all the nations, and then the end will come" (Matt. 24:14). God wants this gospel (good news!) about His Son preached around the world before His return. Therefore we must have money to spread the gospel message. The Bible makes it plain in Romans 10:13–15:

> For "whoever calls on the name of the LORD shall be saved."
> How then shall they call on Him in whom they have not
> believed? And how shall they believe in Him of whom
> they have not heard? And how shall they hear without a
> preacher? And how shall they preach unless they are sent?
> As it is written: "How beautiful are the feet of those who

preach the gospel of peace, who bring glad tidings of good things!"

It is definitely our obligation as the church to send out laborers into the field for the harvest. Now, I believe in equal sacrifice, not necessarily equal giving. The widow woman in Luke 21 gave just two mites into the treasury, yet Jesus said to the disciples, "This poor widow has given more than all the rest of them. For they have given a tiny part of their surplus, but she, poor as she is, has given everything she has" (vv. 3–4, NLT).

Paul admonished Timothy:

> Teach those who are rich in this world not to be proud and not to trust in their money, which is so unreliable. Their trust should be in God, who richly gives us all we need for our enjoyment. Tell them to use their money to do good. They should be rich in good works and generous to those in need, always being ready to share with others. By doing this they will be storing up their treasure as a good foundation for the future so that they may experience true life.
> —1 TIMOTHY 6:17–19, NLT

God wants all of His people to prosper, and He is waiting to bless us beyond our wildest imaginations.

When you read the Book of Ruth, you will find a very interesting word. If you're not careful, you could stumble over it very easily. It is found in Ruth 2:3: "And she went, and came, and gleaned in the field after the reapers: and her *hap* was to light on a part of the field belonging unto Boaz, who was of the kindred of Elimelech" (KJV, emphasis added).

> Do you see that word *hap*? Biblically this word means, "something met with; i.e., an accident or fortune…something befallen…chance…"[5] The word *happen* comes

from this word, and it means, "to take place; come to pass; occur."[6] Think about how many words we use that have *hap* in them, like the phrase, "It just so happened," or "It's happening right now." That three-letter word is found in so many words we use every day, and watch this—*they are all positive.*[7]

The Bible says that Ruth came into her "hap" as she gleaned in the field. So I want to come into agreement and believe with you for your "hap" to come forth, even while you are reading this book. I also agree in Jesus's name that the anointing to prosper will come upon you.

GOD PROSPERS YOU IN EVERY WAY

There are many different ways we can prosper or do kingdom work. Ecclesiastes 10:19 says, "A feast is made for laughter, and wine makes merry; but money answers everything." The necessity of having money is a fact of life. We can all identify with it—because without money we can't eat, keep a roof over our heads, own a car, pay our bills, or do anything! It seems nothing in this world is free. But I have learned that while money "answers everything," *money isn't everything!* There are some things money simply can't buy:

- Your health

- Joy, peace, and righteousness

- A God-kind of happiness

- The anointing of the Lord upon your life

- The presence of God

- Grace and mercy

- Salvation

- Tears of joy and weeping before God in brokenness

- Faith, hope, and love

- And even your godly Boaz or Esther

Most of us have heard a saying throughout our lifetimes that is most often misquoted: "Money is the root of all evil." That's not altogether true. The correct quote, which was spoken by Paul, is: "For the *love of money* is a root of all kinds of evil" (1 Tim. 6:10, emphasis added).

There was one thing that money couldn't buy for Jamie and me at a certain point in our lives, and that was a family. We had been married for four years. We were very happy, but when our two-year wedding anniversary began to roll around, we were feeling that we should start our little family. So we began the process of checking up on our insurance and so on, and we began to pursue getting pregnant. Then we started noticing: months were coming and going, and we still were not pregnant. We began to get concerned.

Finally, after almost a year, we learned that we were *in fact* expecting. We started telling everybody that we were going to have a baby. The flowers came, the cards arrived, and best wishes flowed in to us with congratulations on our soon-to-be new arrival. We were so excited! I knew that I would be having a baby later in my life, but I didn't quite expect it to be *so late*. Nevertheless, we were thrilled. Now, you can't begin to imagine the dismay, the absolute horror, and then the depression that set in on us when we learned that we had miscarried our baby. Our hopes were dashed, and all of our dreams came to a screeching halt.

What in the world happened? The day we found out, we were simply going to hear the baby's heartbeat, so what was the deal? Everything was such a blur when it happened. I could only think, "How could this be?" That tiny baby was just as much a part of me as if I had held him or her in my arms, and to be told that baby was gone was beyond belief. To say we were devastated is a total under-statement. That precious baby was our "firstfruits." Only if you have ever walked that lonely, awful, and despairing road, could you even begin to imagine what it felt like.

We got home that night, and Jamie got me in bed. Then he lay down next to me, and we began to weep together, holding each other at first, and then separating to our opposite sides of the bed to weep in our own way for that which would never be. My husband being the "fixer," as many men are, said to me, "Babe, can I get you something to eat or drink? Can I make you more comfortable? Just please let me do something to make this better."

But we stayed there and just cried. Then he said to me, "Do you mind if I turn on some Christian television? Maybe someone has a word for us tonight." I didn't feel like watching or listening to a program, but I knew it would make him feel better; so we settled in. Jamie got the remote, clicked it on, and immediately Bishop T. D. Jakes came up on the screen.

The Spirit of God began to move, and Bishop Jakes began to speak. He said, "I believe that God has a word for someone tonight." He continued, *"Something has died…"* When he said that, we immediately sat up as straight as we could in our bed, and believe me when I tell you, we were *listening very intently.* He continued, "And your enemy has told you that you will never sing again, preach again, or smile again. But God wants you to know that death is not the end." Then he went on, "You need to tell the devil he is a liar, and God is not finished with you yet."

At this point both of us were crying, screaming "Amen! Hallelujah! Glory!" at the television and declaring the word of the Lord over our lives along with Bishop Jakes. We felt as if someone had gotten ahold of Bishop Jakes and told him everything that was going on, right while he was on the air. I mean, we were so convinced that God was speaking, we could barely breathe.

Bishop Jakes said, "You need to get up on your feet and begin to magnify God and make Him large in your life. And tell the devil, 'It ain't over.'" Believe me when I tell you that the atmosphere in our house changed within a matter of seconds. I looked at my husband and said, "*Run!* That's us he is talking about." My husband jumped up off the bed and then helped me off the bed. I couldn't run, but I sure could walk. While he was running laps of victory up and down the stairs (sometimes you just have to *move* in faith), I was walking back and forth praising God.

If someone had been peeking in our window, they would have thought we had lost our ever-loving minds. We had a word from God, and we needed a miracle. We were not going to miss our moment to seize this word and lay claim on it in the name of the Lord. We knew in the spirit realm that it was already done. Now all we had to do was thank God until our miracle was manifested.

After a while my husband came to me in the bedroom with sweat dripping off of him and asked, "Babe, is that enough running?" It's funny now, but then it was very serious…because we were desperate. Then immediately my husband said, "We have to plant a seed for this child, and we have to get it in the ground tonight." So that is exactly what we did. We wrote checks that emptied all of our bank accounts, giving to ministries we believed were fertile ground. It must have been after midnight, so we had already activated the alarm for our house. We immediately disarmed our alarm system, put stamps on those envelopes, carried them to the mailbox, and put up the little red flag on the side. Then we knew the "seed" was in the ground and our promise was on its way.

It wasn't six months later that we learned we were expecting again. And this time *we knew that we knew* this was our victory! I will never forget holding Judith Kaylee Tuttle in my arms for the first time as Jamie and I cried tears of joy for our little bundle of promise, prophecy, and harvest.

You might ask, "Judy, did that money buy you that child?" Of course not. But I tell you what I do believe: our faith and obedience to do what God had instructed us to do *brought us that child...and another one.*

You see, on the other side of faith and obedience there is a miracle. This is the big takeaway for you for in this chapter. Jesus said, "No one can serve two masters; for either he will hate the one and love the other, or else he will be loyal to the one and despise the other. You cannot serve God and mammon [money]" (Matt. 6:24). Then He went on to say, "'Therefore I say to you, do not worry about your life...'" (v. 25).

The word translated as *worry* here is communicated as "thought" in the King James Version, which comes from the Greek word *merimnaō,* and it means "to be anxious, careful."[8] Another definition reveals that *worry* means "to divide into parts." "This word suggests a distraction, a preoccupation with things causing anxiety, stress, and pressure. Jesus speaks against worry and anxiety because we are under the watchful eye and care of a heavenly Father who is ever mindful of our daily needs."[9]

God does not want us to live in a state of fear, anxiety, and stress. He wants us to live our lives free from poverty, debt, and financial crises. You are anointed to get out of debt. You are anointed to take control of your spending. You are anointed to give generously to the cause of God's kingdom and still be prudent with the resources He has given you. You are anointed to be a good steward of *His* money. *Remember, everything belongs to Him.* I always like to remind our church family when it's time to give: "It is *God's tithe* and *your offering.*" (See Malachi 3:8–12.)

Oh, yes! There is a miracle on the other side of faith and obedience. When we obey the Word of God and walk in His purpose, trusting Him in and through everything we face, He releases His life through us. We experience "greater" in our lives and can do greater works for Him. Now let me go back to the scripture at the beginning of this chapter, this time adding what comes *before* and *after* it:

> But this I say: He who sows sparingly will also reap sparingly, and he who sows bountifully will also reap bountifully. So let each one give as he purposes in his heart, not grudgingly or of necessity; for God loves a cheerful giver. *And God is able to make all grace abound toward you, that you, always having all sufficiency in all things, may have an abundance for every good work....Now may He who supplies seed to the sower, and bread for food, supply and multiply the seed you have sown and increase the fruits of your righteousness, while you are enriched in everything for all liberality, which causes thanksgiving through us to God.*
> —2 Corinthians 9:6–8, 10–11, emphasis added

What Can We Give God for All He's Done for Us?

I pray the anointing to prosper will come upon you so strongly that you will prosper in every way and cause thanksgiving to come back to God. When you really think about it, we could never repay Him for what He has done for us, not in a thousand lifetimes. The psalmist David said in Psalm 116:12, "What shall I render to the LORD for all His benefits toward me?" So the question becomes..."What are His benefits?"

To learn about these blessings, we can go to another psalm of David: Psalm 103. In this song he lays out in no uncertain terms just *some* of the benefits that come from blessing, trusting, and serving God. David starts out in the first verse: "Bless the LORD, O my soul; and all that is within me, bless His holy name!" A popular commentary states:

To bless; to salute, congratulate, thank, praise, and to kneel down....In OT times, one got down on his knees when preparing to speak or receive words of blessing, whether to God in heaven, or to the king on his throne. From God's side, He is the Blesser, the One who gives the capacity for living a full, rich life. The first action of God the Creator to the newly created man and woman was to bless them (Gen. 1:28). In Jewish worship, God is frequently called *ha-Qodesh baruch hu*, or literally, "The Holy One, blessed is He!"[10]

Next, David begins to declare God's benefits:

- "Who forgives all your iniquities" (v. 3). The word *iniquity* speaks of "gross injustice or wickedness...a violation of right or duty; wicked act; sin."[11]

- "Who heals all your diseases" (v. 3). When the Word of God says "all," it means the word *all*. There is a name that is above every sickness and every disease known to man. That name is Jesus.

- "Who redeems your life from destruction" (v. 4). The commentary adds: "...Ransom, redeem, repurchase; to set free by avenging or repaying. [It] refers to the custom of buying back something a person has lost through helplessness, poverty, or violence. Furthermore, the one who does the redeeming is often a close relative who is in a stronger position and buys back the lost property on behalf of his weak relative."[12] (This is such a picture of our elder brother—Jesus.)

- "Who crowns you with lovingkindness and tender mercies" (v. 4). James 5:11 says, "You have heard of Job's perseverance and have seen what the Lord finally brought about. The Lord is full of compassion and mercy" (NIV). God has good things in store for you!

- "Who satisfies your mouth with good things, so that your youth is renewed like the eagle's" (Ps. 103:5).

If I were to ask you when the last time was that you sat down and had a really nice meal, you would probably say, "After church on Sunday with my family," or, "I went out with some friends." Sometime and somewhere you have experienced what it feels like to have your mouth *satisfied with good things*—but God is saying, like David, "Oh, taste and see that the LORD is good" (Ps. 34:8). What God has for you, you've never tasted before. In fact, it is going to take you so high in the spirit realm that you will have to "mount up with wings like eagles" (Isa. 40:31).

WE CAN JOYFULLY GIVE TO GOD WHAT BELONGS TO HIM

Now, let's get back to the question: What could we possibly give to the Lord for all His benefits? Psalm 116:18–19 has the answer: "I will pay my vows to the LORD now in the presence of all His people, in the courts of the LORD's house…"

When you give God what belongs to Him, it releases the anointing to prosper upon your life. And this kind of prosperity is much greater than what the world can give. When God prospers you, it impacts every area of your life. Leviticus 26:9–10 declares, "I will look favorably upon you, making you fertile and multiplying your people. And I will fulfill my covenant with you. You will have such a surplus of crops that you will need to clear out the old grain to make room for the new harvest!" (NLT).

We are anointed to prosper abundantly in this season so the end-time harvest will yield many souls for God! Remember, He honors our faith and humility. No matter what you may be working through, *remember all of His benefits*. Bless God, walk in His purpose, and never stop giving Him your very best. And while you're at it, keep your eyes wide open to everything God has for you. I pray you will be blessed to overflowing!

∞ LET IT BE to ME . . .

The Word of God makes it plain that He wants you to prosper! Living in poverty and lack—broke, busted, and disgusted—is *not* God's plan for you. On the contrary, God has already put it in you to prosper, and Jesus's finished work sealed the fact that as you walk in God's purpose, you will prosper in the Lord. I affirm to you in agreement with the Word of God that He takes pleasure in the prosperity of His servant!

Now, I want you to settle in and meditate on all the ways God has blessed you. Has He healed you—mind, body, and soul? Has He forgiven you when you didn't do things His way? Has He saved you from destruction—spiritually, financially, and otherwise?

Just think about the loving-kindness of the Lord and how He satisfies your mouth with good things! Then take some time to praise Him for what He has done for you. And would you prayerfully consider the following questions? Do you faithfully give the Lord His tithes and your offerings? Do you regularly help others in need? If not, would you take a little time and go through this chapter again? As you do, would you ask the Lord to help you walk in His purpose for your life in this area?

I declare to you: You can't out-give God! I agree with you in the name of Jesus that God will pour out the anointing to prosper upon you and use you mightily in His kingdom purposes! I thank Him for making all grace abound toward you so you have an abundance for every good work, because you are anointed for this!

twelve

MISCONCEPTIONS *and* MISUSES *of the* ANOINTING

For it is the God who commanded light to shine out of dark-
ness, who has shone in our hearts to give the light of the
knowledge of the glory of God in the face of Jesus Christ.
But we have this treasure in earthen vessels, that the excel-
lence of the power may be of God and not of us.

—2 CORINTHIANS 4:6–7

OVER THE CENTURIES people have tried to understand exactly what the anointing is and what they should do with it. Some have linked it with emotion, some with liturgy, and some have even tried to ignore or discount it. In jest, if we were to make a list of "qualifications" for the anointing, it would look something like this:

- You have to be a believer for more than twenty years.

- You have to memorize one hundred Bible verses a week.

- You must have been touched by the latest and greatest evangelist, prophet, or bishop.

- You must have received a prophetic word.

- You must have attended fifteen conferences every month.

- You must fast forty days every year.

As you can see, some of these "qualifications" are a little on the extreme side, but you would be surprised at some teachings people have received throughout their lives...extreme, to say the least. Many of man's requirements are more about "the excellence of the power" being in man rather than it being of God. The Lord doesn't expect you to do these sorts of things to live a life that is anointed by Him and that impacts your world. He just wants your obedience.

You see, man, or should I say, *religious* man, has always tried to explain or logically figure out the anointing. However, like God Himself, the anointing does not fit neatly into anyone's box or framed concept. It is not a trinket that you bedazzle yourself and others with in order to attract people, money, fame, or anything else to your ministry or agenda. The anointing is not based on tradition but will always operate in an environment of *truth*. It is not a showdown of the power of God, but like faith, it expresses itself in *love*.

The anointing is a perfect picture of the power of God coming into our fallen world to make things right again. Jesus proved this point when He quoted the world-changing words from the scroll of Isaiah and emphatically stated, "The Spirit of the Lord is upon Me..." (Luke 4:18–19). And while the Nazareth crowd was staring Him down, He boldly declared, "Today this Scripture is fulfilled in your hearing" (v. 21). Yes, Jesus's words may have almost gotten Him stoned, but they set an atmosphere for the anointing that has endured to this day.

This is *good news*! When Jesus stood up to read, backed by the authority and anointing of heaven, He released life, liberty, healing, and freedom for all time. Why? Because He had been anointed for this! He spoke "Let there be..." over the darkness of His day, and the *truth* confronted lies, strongholds were broken—and everything that was based on the excellence and power of man started shaking.

That's why, decades later, John the beloved would write, "The anointing you received from God abides in you, and you do not need anyone to teach you this.... God's anointing teaches you about everything and is *true* and not a lie, abide in him..." (1 John 2:27, isv). In other words, the anointing—the Holy Spirit of God—is at home in you. He abides, stays, in your inner man! The anointing in your life is not based on whim or emotion. It is a lasting, abiding treasure in your "earthen vessel."

The illuminating power of the anointing will enable you to distinguish between truth and error, between the holy and the profane, so you handle it rightly. And because the anointing is based in *truth*, it faithfully guides and teaches you, bringing you into the fullness of your purpose in God. The anointing is not an act or an event; therefore it cannot be measured by performance. However, the anointing produces results. This may seem like an oxymoron, but remember, the anointing is embodied and fulfilled in the Son of God, the Servant-King, and the Word made flesh, who is both God and man.

WHAT WE DO AND SAY MATTERS TO GOD

A misconception many modern ministers have is that because they are "anointed," their behavior doesn't matter. This is a false assumption and a lie from the pit of hell. How we conduct ourselves before God and man does matter. Paul said in Philippians 3:17–20, "Pattern your lives after mine.... I say it again with tears in my eyes, that there are many whose conduct shows they are really enemies of the cross of Christ.... Their god is their appetite, they brag about shameful things, and they think only about this life here on earth. But we are citizens of heaven, where the Lord Jesus Christ lives" (NLT).

The anointing flows to us from the Holy Spirit, the Spirit of truth, and *truth*—like the light God released at the beginning of Creation—exposes darkness. As we will see later in this chapter, there are serious consequences when one misuses the anointing. Christianity is more than a concept. It affects our behavior, and it affects the lives of other people who are watching us as leaders. James went as far as to say that many should not even desire to be leaders, or teachers, because leaders are held to a stricter standard of judgment (James 3:1).

But through the power of Christ's anointing we can walk worthy of the calling we have received. (See Ephesians 4:1.) Let's do a little exercise, because as I have said from the beginning, if you *say* it you will *see* it!

First of all, the anointing has the ability to make you shine. Remember, it is represented by oil. Moses had to cover his face because it shone so brightly from being in the presence of God (Exod. 34:29–35). The psalmist could say, "You anoint my head with oil" (Ps. 23:5). As a shepherd, David would have anointed his sheep. Sheep were anointed for the same reasons we need the anointing—life is *for real,* and sometimes we get bruised, battered, or even bitten. Oil was used to soothe pain and help heal wounds. And how many believers need the oil of gladness? God gives us the ability to put on the "garment of praise for the spirit of heaviness" (Isa. 61:3), because according to Nehemiah 8:10, the joy of the Lord is our strength. In many ways, the oil of the anointing makes us shine. Say to the Lord right now: "Thank You for anointing me, healing me, strengthening me, and putting a song of praise in my heart. God, thank You for releasing the oil of true worship upon my life by the power of Your anointing. I will rise, shine, and bless You with everything that is in me! Amen!"

Secondly, the anointing has the ability to make you see. Remember, oil was the main ingredient for light in the Old Testament tabernacle. When you have light, you can see. Furthermore, Jesus admonished the church in Laodicea to "anoint your eyes with eye salve, that you may see" (Rev. 3:18). Today, more than ever, we need the ability to *see.* God told Joshua, "See! I have given Jericho into your hand, its king, and the mighty men of valor" (Josh. 6:1). Joshua and the children of Israel had to *see* themselves in the spirit realm, first of all, bringing down those city walls with a shout. In like manner, you have to see yourself *when* (not if) your enemy is defeated and *what* the victory is going to look like as you celebrate! *Do you see this?* Do you see that child off drugs? Do you see that marriage restored to how things were when you first dated? Do you see yourself out of debt? Do you see your finances restored or your body healed? Do you see yourself being set free to truly be free? You have to see the victory!

Another example of *seeing* is when Elisha prayed when the king of Syria and his army were coming against him and his servant. The servant was obviously beyond nervous; he was just plain ol' scared. I can just imagine the prophet sitting on the porch drinking a cold glass of tea. The prophet told the Lord, "I pray thee, open his eyes, that he may see. And the LORD opened the eyes of the young man; and he saw: and, behold, the mountain was full of horses and chariots of fire round about Elisha" (2 Kings 6:17, KJV). If you lack the insight to see, then let's go before the Lord together and *say,* "Lord, thank You for anointing us with insight from Your perspective in the now of life and for giving us anointed foresight for what is coming in the future. We thank You that from this day forward we will *see* the victory. In Jesus's name, amen!"

Next, the anointing has the ability to sanctify. Everything the anointing oil touched was pronounced holy and was set apart for the Master's use. I can remember the old saints in my church singing a song that went something like this:

Nothing but the pure gold in that city
Nothing but the pure gold in that city
Nothing but the pure gold in that city
Oh, my Lord, make me pure.

If you ask the Lord to consecrate you, He will do it, but He needs you to fully cooperate with Him. By the power of the Holy Spirit you must take control of your flesh and tell it, "Jesus is Lord, not you!" The Bible says, "Cleanse yourselves and be clean, you who bear the vessels of the Lord" (Isa. 52:11, AMP). God wants His people to be pure and holy, for He is pure and holy. David said, "Who shall ascend the hill of the LORD? or who shall stand in his holy place? He that hath clean hands, and a pure heart" (Ps. 24:3–4, KJV). So let's *say* to the Lord right now: "Gracious Father, we receive Your anointing afresh that sets us apart for Your kingdom work. We confess our sins to You [name them if you need to]. Thank You for forgiving and cleansing us. Lord, thank You that because You are holy, we are holy. We bless You for setting us apart to walk worthy of our calling in the name of Jesus! Amen."

Fourthly, the anointing has the ability to set you free. God encouraged the remnant of Israel, "In that day…his burden will be taken away from your shoulder, and his yoke from your neck.… [It] will be destroyed because of the anointing oil" (Isa. 10:27). In the natural God was talking to Israel about the Assyrians. In the spirit realm Jesus came and destroyed the works of our enemy, the devil! That is why, once again, He read that scroll in Nazareth, declaring from that day forward it was fulfilled in their hearing. The devil hates and has always hated freedom. He wants to keep us bound, chained, down and out, and lost and undone. He doesn't want us to be joyful, walking in peace and contentment, but Jesus came to set the captives free. In fact, He guarantees that if you will trust Him as your Redeemer, Savior, and the one who gives you the ability and the anointing to be free, "then you are unquestionably free" (John 8:36, MOFFATT).

You had better get ready, because the anointing that is coming on you is going to be so strong, everything that comes in your path is going to be moved out of the way. Oh, yes! The anointing in you is going to annihilate the enemy's strategy against you. Say with me: "Jesus, You are a mighty deliverer! I thank You that I am *free indeed* and that no weapon formed against me will prosper all the days of my life, because of the power of Your anointing! I bless You, worship You, and will serve You all of my days, for You have destroyed the enemy's power over my life. Amen."

Lastly, the anointing has the ability to enable you to stand. Paul writes in 2 Corinthians 1:21, "But it is God Who confirms and makes us steadfast and establishes us [in joint fellowship]...and has consecrated and anointed us [enduing us with the gifts of the Holy Spirit]" (AMP). In my book *Stand Strong* I tell readers that our position before God is to stand before Him in faith, boldness, determination, authority, worship, and praise. That is our posture, position, and stance. The devil would have you to sit down on the promises of God, the prophecies spoken over you, your family, your marriage, and your ministry. Having done all to stand, you will stand. Now, keeping your eyes fixed on Jesus, set your face like flint and say: "Jesus, because You have anointed me, I will be determined. I will win this thing! I will stand strong through the power of Your anointing, flow in the gifts You have given me, and do greater works in Your kingdom...all for Your glory! Amen."

I declare the anointing will flow through you like a mighty river of truth in these last days! I say that you will *say yes* to God as a yielded, holy vessel from this day forward by the excellent power of the Holy Spirit—because in the times we are living in, nothing less than the true, pure, authentic anointing of God will get the job done.

We Can't "Fake" the Anointing

Let's remember 2 Corinthians 10:4–5:

> For the weapons of our warfare are not carnal but mighty in God for pulling down strongholds, casting down arguments and every high thing [*including demonic principalities!*] that exalts itself against the knowledge of God, bringing every thought into captivity to the obedience of Christ, and being ready to punish all disobedience when your obedience is fulfilled.

God knows our hearts and discerns our motives, whether they are pure or not. We can't fool God or play games with the anointing. We can't "fake" the anointing. There is an old saying attributed to Abraham Lincoln: "You may fool all of the people some of the time; you can even fool some of the people all of the time; but you can't fool all of the people all of the time."[1] The Bible makes it clear that you can't fool the spiritual kingdom with a fake anointing. The Spirit of God can't be moved by decibels or by demonstration. *In other words, no matter how loud you shout or how theatrical you are, it is the anointing that breaks the yoke and sets the captives free.* The anointing of the Lord is authentic. It is not a copycat power, nor is it a magic charm or incantation.

Ask the seven sons of Sceva about this. Acts 19:11 records that "unusual miracles," such as healings and deliverances, occurred as the anointing flowed through Paul (and even through handkerchiefs and aprons he had touched). When the sons of Sceva decided to attempt this, calling on the name of Jesus, "whom Paul preaches" (vv. 13–14), it created a violent, demonic response.

The evil spirit answered, "Jesus I know, and Paul I know; but who are you?" Then the man in whom the evil spirit was leaped on them, overpowered them, and *prevailed* against them, so that they fled out of that house naked and wounded.

—ACTS 19:15–16, EMPHASIS ADDED

If you play with fire (even profane fire), you will get burned. *How humiliating!*

There was a positive outcome, however, because this became widely known, "and the name of the Lord Jesus was magnified" (v. 17). How great is our God! This incident also led to revival—verse 19 says people brought their magic paraphernalia and "burned them in the sight of all." Every single time, what the enemy does for evil, God turns it around for good.

You may be thinking, "Well, *they* deserved that, but I don't play around with magic." Take in the words of one of today's modern prophets, Iverna Tompkins, as she explains the profane. In her book *The Holy and the Profane* she relates that most people assume that profanity is taking the Lord's name in vain, or that it's some outwardly immoral act. She goes on to say, "Profanity, in God's sight, is anything which deals lightly with what He calls holy."[2]

Most of what goes on in our world today would be considered "profane" to God. We are living in the days in which Isaiah describes where society calls evil good and calls good evil. Anyone who stands up for righteousness and is against abortion or same-sex marriage is deemed a right-wing extremist and archaic, with the possibility of facing hate crime charges.

Iverna goes on to say, "The first step of progression in profanity is indifference."[3] Years ago Doris Day used to sing a song titled "Que Sera Sera," which means that if something is to be, it will be. I beg to differ! This is not a theme song for the church of the living God. I *say* we are the men and women of Issachar: we know the times and we know what to do. (See 1 Chronicles 12:32.) We will not settle. We will use our voices, our vote, God's money (not ours), prayer, and the Word of the living God. We will affect this culture for the sake of those who have fought, bled, and died a martyr's death, especially the beautiful Lamb who was slain. We can call forth those things that *be not* as though they *are*, in Jesus's name! (See Romans 4:17.)

Iverna then goes on to explain, "The second step toward a *profane spirit* is…*injury. Indifference leads to hostility.* A neutral position progresses to hostile feelings as we defend our positions….*If I become hostile, I will injure.*"[4] She continues, "A profane spirit continues from injury to insult. In fact, insult is the most characteristic mark of a *profane spirit.*"[5] The one thing that will win this world is our love. Why? The Word says, "By this all will know that you are My disciples, if you have love for one another" (John 13:35).

Psalm 24 asks, "Who may ascend into the hill of the Lord…who may stand in His holy place?" David then answers, "He who has clean hands and a pure heart, who has not lifted up his soul to an idol, nor sworn deceitfully" (vv. 3–4). Songwriter, recording artist, and worship leader Martha Munizzi, chimes in:

> True anointing comes from a brokenness at the cross. When we are broken, that's when the anointing of God transforms us and then flows out of us to change the world. Many believers don't know the difference between anointing and gifting. Gifting causes you to want to know more about the one who is gifted. Anointing causes you to want to know more about Jesus.[6]

Thus, we must treasure the Anointed One and the anointing He gives us to fulfill His purposes for His kingdom. We must deem the anointing as something precious, something pure, and something to be kept and guarded at all times. But more importantly, it is to be shared. Why? Because God gave us His anointing to change the world.

Recently I was visiting the Smithsonian's National Museum of Natural History with some friends in Washington DC. As we were going through the museum, I came across the Hope diamond, which was encased in the middle of the room. It weighs almost 46 carats, and the chain of the necklace itself embodies sixteen white diamonds.[7]

As I was walking around the encasing, along with five or six other people who were trying to see it amongst people who were taking pictures of it, I noticed people just standing there gazing at it. They were in awe of what had happened in nature to bring forth something so amazing. Then I couldn't help but notice there were at least four guards visible to the eyes, not counting the cameras that were in seclusion, guarding one of the world's greatest possessions.

At that moment I thought about the anointing upon my life and how I have to always protect it. I must have my guard up at all times and never let anything come between me and the Spirit of God who gives the anointing. I must stand watch and guard against the enemy who comes to steal, kill, and destroy that which is more precious than silver, gold, or any diamond of any size.

Not only must we guard with all diligence the anointing upon our lives, but we also must keep our hearts and spirits pure—for the anointing is holy and we are holy unto the Lord. When we flow in our God-given anointing, we are indeed salt and light to our society (Matt. 5:13–16). Salt is a preserving agent. Light dispels the darkness. However, there is a cost factor involved for carrying the anointing. We must worship the Lord "in the beauty of holiness" (1 Chron. 16:29).

Pastor Desmond Evans says, "It would be much easier to worship Him in the bounty of our giving, or in the bigness of our programs, or even in the blessing of His power, but He says [we are to worship Him] in the BEAUTY OF HOLINESS."[8]

There Are Consequences for Abusing the Anointing

There are countless examples in the Bible where the anointing was abused and the consequences were severe. Nadab and Abihu, sons of Aaron, were priests who offered "profane fire" before the Lord. They were instantly devoured by fire and died. (See Leviticus 10:1–2.) The word *profane* ("strange," KJV) comes from the Hebrew word *zûr* (pronounced "zoor"), which means, "to turn aside...to be a foreigner, strange, profane...to commit adultery."[9] Together, the words *strange* (*zûr*) *fire* (*zûr ʾēsh* [pronounced "aysh"][10]) are seen by scholars as making reference to idolatrous worship.

Nadab and Abihu had taken fire for their censers from a place other than the altar, which means they did not do things according to the pattern. As we covered in chapter 2, God is specific about how He wants things to be done, because He does everything with purpose.

Furthermore, ancient Jewish interpretation suggests that they were intoxicated.[11] The stern rebuke of the Lord declared, "By those who come near Me I must be regarded as holy; and before all the people I must be glorified" (Lev. 10:3). Their father, Aaron, was not allowed to take off his priestly garments or even leave the tabernacle because "the anointing oil of the LORD" was upon him (vv. 6–7). Wow. We must respect the anointing and guard it at all costs.

Most believers see Ezekiel 28:12–15, 17 as being indicative of the fall of Lucifer, who was the anointed musician and worship leader in heaven. Read these verses with me:

> You were the seal of perfection, full of wisdom and perfect in beauty. You were in Eden, the garden of God; every precious stone was your covering: the sardius, topaz, and

diamond, beryl, onyx, and jasper, sapphire, turquoise, and emerald with gold. The workmanship of your timbrels and pipes was prepared for you on the day you were created. You were the anointed cherub who covers; I established you; you were on the holy mountain of God; you walked back and forth in the midst of fiery stones. You were perfect in your ways from the day you were created, till iniquity was found in you.... Your heart was lifted up because of your beauty.

How severe and swift was God's judgment on Lucifer? He was cast out of heaven down to earth, along with angels who sinned with him (Rev. 12:9). And being enraged, he makes war with those who keep God's commandments and have the testimony of Jesus Christ (Rev. 12:17). Jesus said, "I saw Satan fall like lightning from heaven" (Luke 10:18). That, my friend, is swift justice.

Simon the sorcerer sought to buy the anointing (Acts 8:13–19). But Peter sternly rebuked him, saying, "Your money perish with you, because you thought that the gift of God could be purchased with money! You have neither part nor portion in this matter, for your heart is not right in the sight of God.... For I see that you are poisoned by bitterness and bound by iniquity" (vv. 20–23). Once again there was no hesitation when guarding the priceless value of the anointing.

One of the things we have to constantly be on guard against is "the accuser of the brethren." He accuses us before our Lord "day and night" (Rev. 12:10). And he will try to accuse you of every little thing you say, think, feel, do, or even imagine. He is there to keep you constantly in fear, doubt, unbelief, and condemnation. Remember, God never condemns you (John 3:17). The Holy Spirit will convict you (John 16:8–11), but He will never condemn you.

You have to discern, with the help of the Holy Spirit, which voice to hear and obey. If you feel bad, rotten, worthless, and hopeless, that's not God; that is the accuser of the brethren. It is at that moment when you have to "submit to God. Resist the devil and he will flee" (James 4:7).

Now, if there is something you need to repent of, the Holy Spirit will deal with you on that level. You will hear a voice behind you saying, "This is the way, walk in it" (Isa. 30:21).

WE MUST BELIEVE GOD AND FLOW IN THE ANOINTING...*RIGHTLY*

Misuse of the anointing, however, is no excuse for *non-use*. What's needed today is *correct use*. Songwriter, worship pastor, international worship teacher and leader Wes Tuttle states:

> I find that I use the word *anointed* rather sparingly. The reason is that I have such a reverence for what it means that I do not want to be careless or flippant in its use. Frankly, I recognize that my assessment of what is "anointed" is inconsequential. Biblical anointing is and always has been the work of the Holy Spirit. He is the one who determines whom or what is anointed. And His assessment is the only one that matters.
>
> It is evident in the Scriptures that biblical anointing is related to one's being set apart or consecrated to a particular calling, work, service, or ministry. For example, when Samuel anointed David as king of Israel in 1 Samuel 16, David was set apart to fulfill the will and purposes of God. The anointing was not to advance David's agenda but God's. God's anointing upon us is for His kingdom's advancement, not ours.
>
> In Luke 4 Jesus stood in the synagogue in Nazareth, read from Isaiah 61, and interpreted the passage as having been fulfilled in Himself. "The Spirit of the Lord is upon Me, because He has anointed Me...": Jesus, the Messiah,

the Anointed One. Perhaps the most defining character-istic of what it means to be anointed is "Christlikeness." In other words, a person who is anointed by the Holy Spirit will, to borrow a phrase from Oswald Chambers, bear an "unmistakable family resemblance to Jesus Christ"[12]...the Anointed One.[13]

The disciples had walked so closely with Jesus for so long they were comfortable flowing in the anointing and diligent guarding it. When the anointing flowed through the ministry of Paul and Barnabus, resulting in the healing of a crippled man in Lystra, the people (including the priest of Zeus) wanted to sacrifice to them and called them gods (Acts 14:8–13). Paul responded by saying, "Men, why are you doing these things? We also are men with the same nature as you, and preach to you that you should turn from these useless things to the living God, who made the heaven, the earth, the sea, and all things that are in them" (v. 15).

The examples in the Bible are written for our admonition (1 Cor. 10:11). We are to walk in His anointing and fulfill our calling as unto the Lord, whatever that calling may be. According to Hebrews 13:21, He will equip you in every good work to do His will. Why? *We have priceless treasure in our earthen vessels.* So, just as Paul warned Timothy, I urge you to "guard what was committed to your trust, avoiding the profane and idle babblings and contradictions of what is falsely called knowledge" (1 Tim. 6:20). Guard the anointing the Lord has invested in you...it is more precious than gold. It is even more precious than the Hope diamond. Why? Because "we have this treasure in earthen vessels, that the excellence of the power may be of God and not of us" (2 Cor. 4:7).

I love this note that was given to me by Cheryl Gesing of Undiscovered Treasure Ministries. It sums up what we have been learning about the anointing beautifully. Cheryl shares with us:

The anointing is a holy thing...a mystery...a necessary tool for a righteous person. We are called to be kings and priests unto God...if this is so, the anointing is a *must*. The first mention of anointing in God's Word is found in Exodus 28:41, where God informs Moses that those who serve and minister to Him must be anointed, consecrated, and sanctified. The definitions tell us this: if we want to serve and minister to God, we must be rubbed with the oil of His Holy Spirit, be wholly situated in the mighty right hand of God, where all power and dominion is situated, and be physically and spiritually holy. The anointing gives us the ability to use the dominion of Jesus over the realm of the adversary. As we tear down the gates of the enemy's strongholds, the anointing brings us deliverance from enemies, personal safety, strength, answers to our prayers, mercy, gladness, and is a light in dark places.

Jesus is the head of the body of Christ. He was anointed as our example. When oil is poured onto the head, it runs down to the body. His anointing is our anointing...His ministry is our ministry...His anointing enables us to continue His ministry statement:

"The Spirit of the Lord GOD is upon Me, because the LORD has anointed Me to preach good tidings to the poor; He has sent Me to heal the brokenhearted, to proclaim liberty to the captives, and the opening of the prison to those who are bound; to proclaim the acceptable year of the LORD, and the day of vengeance of our God; to comfort all who mourn, to console those who mourn in Zion, to give them beauty for ashes, the oil of joy for mourning, the garment of praise for the spirit of heaviness; that they may be called trees of righteousness, the planting of the LORD, that He may be glorified" (Isa. 61:1–3).

Remember as you go and do...God made you unique. Your anointing is specific to your personality and giftings.

Each anointing is different. Don't be intimidated when you look at Judy's; walk yours out with boldness! Finish the work Jesus began...take *His* presence where only *you* can! Shalom...[14]

⊚ LET IT BE to ME...

I have loved taking this journey with you to help you discover that you—*yes, you*—are anointed of God. This chapter might just be the "meatiest" of all, because the Lord's instructions about guarding His anointing aren't for the feeble in heart. But there is a mighty promise for those who honor and obey His Word, which, as you know, is our final authority. In Psalm 19 David testified about the law, the testimony, the statutes, the commandment, and the fear of the Lord (vv. 7–9). Then He declared, "More to be desired are they than gold, yea, than much fine gold; sweeter also than honey and the honeycomb." And here's the promise: "Moreover by them Your servant is warned, and in keeping them there is great reward" (vv. 10–11).

Since we've already done an exercise earlier in this chapter, let me ask this of you: as you continue walking in the anointing, make it a daily priority to commit the Word of God to your heart. If you would, I want you to make a special effort to memorize the main verses in this book, which are in the Introduction and at the beginning of every chapter.

Make it your priority to know the "Let there be..." God has spoken over His people (corporately) and you (personally). Then boldly declare, "Let it be to me according to Your Word." I declare and agree that as you *say* what God has purposed for your life, you will *see* His purpose come to pass...because you are anointed for this!

Conclusion

STAYING *in the* FLOW *of the* ANOINTING

[May] the God of our Lord Jesus Christ, the Father of glory... give to you the spirit of wisdom and revelation in the knowledge of Him, the eyes of your understanding being enlightened; that you may know what is the hope of His calling, what are the riches of the glory of His inheritance in the saints, and what is the exceeding greatness of His power toward us who believe, according to the working of His mighty power.

—EPHESIANS 1:17–19

NOT TOO LONG ago I visited one of my favorite spots in the Great Smoky Mountains to do some writing for this book. On such a beautiful day and on such a lovely property, we were getting away for a few days. It is a beautiful resort that our family loves to visit and just relax. One of my favorite things about this spot is a small river stream that goes alongside of the property. My daughter Erica loves to skip rocks on the water. (Thank you, Mr. Williams!) She also loves to see how many skips she can get in before the rock sinks to the bottom. Well, as soon as we arrived on the property, Erica said to me, "Come on, Mom, let's go skip rocks on the river while Dad and KK check in." So I agreed.

On the banks of this little river stream there are two paths: one for people and one for animals. The path for people is perfect for those late-night strolls or just to enjoy a nice walk beside the stream to get your heart rate up. The other path is for pets...and that is all I am going to say about that. (I think you know what it is used for!)

That weekend Erica was sporting a brand-new pair of tennis shoes, and so I warned her, "Erica, stay on this path. Don't get up there on the pet path; you know what will happen." So off she went, looking and looking for just the right smooth stone. She finally found one, but in the meantime, she found something else. "Mom!" she cried as she ran up to me, "Yuk! Help, Mom! Look at the bottom of my tennis shoes. They're brand-new..." So you know what I was doing for the rest of the night. Exactly. Cleaning poop off tennis shoes.

What's my point? We know what God's path looks like, and we know the right thing to do is to stay on the path that God has mapped out for us. If we veer off to the right or to the left, in our own minds we think we will catch up. But we must be careful. One of the saddest commentaries found in the New Testament is in Paul's letter to Timothy. He said to him, "Be diligent to come to me quickly; for Demas *has forsaken me*, having loved this present world, and has departed for Thessalonica" (2 Tim. 4:9–10, emphasis added). Whatever happened with Demas didn't happen overnight, but little by little Demas kept looking over his shoulder until finally he abandoned his call.

STAY ON THE PATH OF THE ANOINTING

I got smack-dab in the middle of this book, and it began to dawn on me how inexhaustible a title on the subject of the anointing can be.

I thought to myself, "If I were reading a book like this and was finishing up, what would I want to take away from it?" I thought about several things: Perry's foreword, Pastor Parsley's endorsement, along with the contributions of many other anointed men and women of God. I thought, "Yes, it is absolutely important to guard it. There must be an unction from the Holy One to even operate in it, and if you don't know how to do warfare and fight, it is already an uphill climb."

So what is going to make this thing in us called "the anointing" last until Jesus comes back? And after that, continue enjoying it throughout all eternity with the Anointed One? *We must stay on the path.* What do I mean by staying on the path? Solomon put it very simply, "A sensible person stays on the right path" (Prov. 15:21, NLT).

Jesus said, "Enter by the narrow gate; for wide is the gate and broad is the way that leads to destruction, and there are many who go in by it. Because narrow is the gate and difficult is the way which leads to life, and there are few who find it" (Matt. 7:13–14).

It is so crucial to do all the things that seemingly are so simple but yet so dire. So many have gotten off the path and have caused so much pain, grief, and confusion. I have found there are basically three things that are basic to keeping the flow of the anointing in your life.

Stay on the path of reading the Word of God

David said to the Lord, "Your Word I have hidden in my heart, that I might not sin against You!" (Ps. 119:11). And He declared, "Your Word is a lamp to my feet and a light to my path" (v. 105).

Again, the Word is our final authority, and when our lives don't measure up with the Word, everything else will be misaligned. I don't care what title is in front of your name or who you are, "let him who thinks he stands take heed lest he fall" (1 Cor. 10:12). The Word keeps everything in balance in our lives.

Stay on the path of prayer

As we have learned, prayer is the fuel that keeps the engine of the Holy Spirit revved up in your life. Apart from communication with

God, you are as "a sounding brass or a clanging cymbal" (1 Cor. 13:1). Prayer is the most powerful thing on this planet. Jesus commanded His disciples, "Watch and pray" (Matt. 26:41). In the hour that we are living in, we must be "wise as serpents and harmless as doves" (Matt. 10:16). We must be wide-awake to know the mind of God and be able to move with His instructions for these last days. God is looking for someone who will stand in the gap. A prayerless Christian is a powerless Christian. "No prayer, no power: know prayer, know power!"

Stay on the path by being in church

There is a reason the writer of Hebrews says:

> And let us consider and give attentive, continuous care to watching over one another, studying how we may stir up (stimulate and incite) to love and helpful deeds and noble activities, not forsaking or neglecting to assemble together [as believers], as is the habit of some people, but admonishing (warning, urging, and encouraging) one another, and all the more faithfully as you see the day approaching.
> —Hebrews 10:24–25, AMP

It is important that you stay in church, and not only that, but also be involved in church. Find out where your giftings and anointing fit and serve there. Celebrate your pastors and pray for them, "for they watch out for your souls" (Heb. 13:17).

You *cannot* live a successful Christian life and stay in the anointing unless you stay on the path of what God has ordained for His church. *The truth of the matter is this: I need you, and you need me.* You will not get a television to hug you back, I don't care how many times you place your hand on it or on a computer screen. You need to be under the umbrella of a pastor, a man and/or woman of God who will love you, protect you, encourage you, and visit you if you or your loved ones are in need. Romans 10:17

says, "Faith comes by hearing, and hearing by the word of God." Receiving an anointed word from a man or woman of God is just how God set things up.

We must stay on God's path to walk consistently in the anointing. Now is the time to "live soberly, righteously, and godly in the present age" (Titus 2:12). Hebrews 13:18 encourages us, "Live honorably." Peter said, "Live according to God in the spirit" (1 Pet. 4:6), which means living with eternal life in view.

THE OIL OF THE ANOINTING IS UPON YOU

At the end of Jonathan Cahn's best-selling book *The Harbinger,* Nouriel Kaplan (the main character) has been telling a media executive, Ana Goren, his amazing story about his encounters with a prophet from God. In his last session with her, Nouriel tells her about his final conversation with God's messenger, when he had confided to him:

> "Still, I don't feel adequate, not remotely adequate for anything like this."
>
> "How do you think Moses felt when he was called, or Jeremiah....or Mary...or Peter? Do you think any of them felt remotely adequate? It wasn't about them. And it's not about you. It's about Him. All you have to do is go where He sends you." Then he reached into his coat and took out a little horn...a little ram's horn. "Close your eyes, Nouriel," he said, lifting the horn above my head.
>
> So I did. I soon felt a thick liquid rolling down my forehead.

Then the story shifts back to the office where Nouriel and Ana are talking.

> "It was oil?" she asked.

"Yes, I think olive oil."
"A horn of oil."
"The oil of anointing…"[1]

I don't know if you have read *The Harbinger,* but Nouriel had to walk a very specific path that was revealed to him by the prophet. Otherwise, the mystery that was unfolded to him might never have played out.

Stay on the path of God's anointing. The anointing is upon you, but staying the path—*staying the course*—is the only way His oil will continue to flow *to you* and *through you.* It is the only way the world will see *and* experience the exceeding greatness of His power as you obey the Lord and walk in His anointing. I love the words of a good friend of ours in ministry, who is intimately acquainted with the anointing:

First John 2:27 suggests that the Holy Spirit operates on a variety of levels, and each level reproduces its own unique kind of fruit. The blessed Holy Spirit is not only the anointer, but He is also the anointing.

- *He is the atmosphere,* which enables us to *stand* in newness of life.
- *He is the ability,* which enables us to *succeed* even when facing unbelievable odds and circumstances.
- *He is the agent,* which enables us to *soar beyond* the three-dimensional restrictions of time and space.
- *He is the activator,* which enables us to *sanctify* the sinful environment of our day.
- *He is the ambassador,* which enables us *to speak authoritatively* to principalities and powers in the name [of Jesus].

- *He is the authority*, which enables us to *see beyond* the obvious in order to increase one's spiritual well-being and faith.[2]

—DES EVANS
PASTOR EMERITUS, BETHESDA COMMUNITY CHURCH

I urge you: don't just jump into the river of the anointing... dive as deeply in those holy waters as God will lead you. Keep following Him, and never look back. One day you will *see* the most amazing river of all flowing from New Jerusalem. Revelation 22:1–2 says, "And he showed me a pure river of water of life, clear as crystal, proceeding from the throne of God and of the Lamb. In the middle of its street, and on either side of the river, was the tree of life, which bore twelve fruits, each tree yielding its fruit every month. The leaves of the tree were for the healing of the nations."

Amen! And I *say*, "Let healing spring forth even now as we flow in the anointing." Jesus declared, "If anyone thirsts, let him come to Me and drink. He who believes in Me, as the Scripture has said, out of his heart will flow rivers of living water" (John 7:37–38). He was speaking of the Holy Spirit. The Bible says many believed that day, but some of the people doubted Him. Then everything started stirring up; I guess you could say it turned into a paradoxical situation. But as you know, from the beginning this is how God releases His anointing.

So rise up and go under the unction of the Lord. Do what He has called, anointed, and gifted you to accomplish for such a time as this! Remember, you will never discover new oceans until you are willing to lose sight of the shore. You are not by yourself. Emmanuel—the Son of man, Son of God, and Servant-King—is with you!

Since you met Jesus, and certainly while you have been reading this book, God has been leading you through a "this" so He can get you to a "that." Oh, yes! Because, as I stated in the beginning of this book, "*this* is *that* which was spoken by the prophet Joel" (Acts 2:16, KJV, emphasis added). God is pouring out His Spirit so you can go to a place in the spirit realm where you have always longed to go. And you can dwell in that place, in the anointing, and change your atmosphere, yes, even your culture, for the glory of God.

So, stand strong, stay on the path, and keep pressing toward the prize! Run to win this race. *I declare to you right now: You shall do greater works in the name of Jesus! Rivers of living water shall flow from within you and bring healing wherever you go, because the master mentor of all time has already gone before you. All things are possible, my friend, because you are anointed for this!*

NOTES

INTRODUCTION—GOD'S ANOINTING IS FOR YOU

1. Harry R. Jackson Jr. and Tony Perkins, *Personal Faith, Public Policy* (Lake Mary, FL: FrontLine, 2008), vii.

CHAPTER 1—IN THE BEGINNING

1. *Strong's Talking Greek and Hebrew Dictionary*, s.v. "kābôd," OT:3519, WORDSearch 7.0, copyright © 2007, WORDSearch Corporation. All rights reserved.

CHAPTER 2—WHAT IS THE ANOINTING?

1. Written by Jamie Tuttle specifically for this book.
2. *Merriam-Webster's Collegiate Dictionary*, 11th edition (Sprinfield, MA: Merriam-Webster, Inc., 2003), s.v. "archetype."
3. *Strong's Talking Greek and Hebrew Dictionary*, s.v. "māshah," OT:4886.
4. Ibid., s.v. "mishhâ," OT:4888.
5. *Vine's Expository Dictionary of Old and New Testament Words*, s.v. "māshah," WORDsearch 7.0. Copyright © 2007 WORDsearch Corp. All rights reserved.
6. Bible Suite, *Clarke's Commentary on the Bible*, s.v. "Exodus 30:23," http://bible.cc/exodus/30-23.htm (accessed April 23, 2013).
7. M. G. Easton, *Illustrated Bible Dictionary*, s.v. "frankincense," BibleStudyTools.com, http://www.biblestudytools.com/dictionaries/eastons-bible-dictionary/frankincense.html (accessed April 23, 2013).
8. *Strong's Talking Greek and Hebrew Dictionary*, s.v. "mishhâ," OT:4888, and s.v. "māshîah," OT:4899.
9. Bill Bright, *Discover the Book God Wrote* (Wheaton, IL: Tyndale House Publishers, 2005), 177.
10. P. G. Matthew, "Imageo Deo, Part 2," sermon preached May 13, 2001, GraceValley.org, http://www.gracevalley.org/sermon_trans/2001/Imago_Dei_2.html (accessed April 23, 2013).

CHAPTER 3—YOU ARE ANOINTED FOR THIS

1. "Tafawa Balewa Square," http://www.lgtnigeria.com/viewListing_page.php?id=418 (accessed April 5, 2013).

211

2. *Webster's American Family Dictionary* (New York: Random House, 1998), s.v. "prepare."
3. Martin Luther King Jr., *The Autobiography of Martin Luther King, Jr.*, Clayborne Carson, ed. (New York: Warner Books, 1998), 9.
4. Written by Amanda Fisher specifically for this book.
5. Cindy Trimm, *Commanding Your Morning* (Lake Mary, FL: Charisma House, 2007), 121–123.

CHAPTER 4—THE ANOINTING OF TRUE WORSHIP

1. Archives.gov, "The Charters of Freedom: Bill of Rights," http://www.archives.gov/exhibits/charters/bill_of_rights_transcript.html (accessed April 8, 2013).
2. "Mount Vernon," OldTownAlexandria.net, http://www.oldtownalexandria.net/mount-vernon/ (accessed May 13, 2013).
3. Jack Hayford, *Prayer Is Invading the Impossible* (Alachua, FL: Bridge-Logos Publishers, 1977), 105. Viewed at Google Books.
4. *Strong's Talking Greek and Hebrew Dictionary*, s.v. "dunamis," NT:1411.

CHAPTER 5—THE ANOINTED PRAY-ER

1. Oswald Chambers, *My Utmost for His Highest* (Uhrichsville, OH: Discovery House, 1992), "February 7."
2. *Strong's Talking Greek and Hebrew Dictionary*, s.v. "justified, dikaioo," NT:1344.
3. Robert J. Morgan, *100 Bible Verses Everyone Should Know by Heart* (Nashville: B&H Publishing Group, 2010), 17. Viewed at Google Books.
4. BibleGateway.com, *IVP New Testament Commentaries*, s.v. "John 11," http://www.biblegateway.com/resources/commentaries/IVP-NT/John/Jesus-Raises-Lazarus (accessed April 8, 2013).
5. Written by Mary Alessi specifically for this book.
6. Biblesoft's *New Exhaustive Strong's Numbers and Concordance with Expanded Greek-Hebrew Dictionary*, copyright © 1994 Biblesoft and International Bible Translators, Inc., s.v. "proseuchomai," NT:4336.
7. Hayford, *Prayer Is Invading the Impossible*, 6. Viewed at Google Books.
8. Biblesoft's *New Exhaustive Strong's Numbers and Concordance with Expanded Greek-Hebrew Dictionary*, s.v. "euchomai," NT:2172.

9. Hayford, *Prayer Is Invading the Impossible*, 144. Viewed at Google Books.

10. Biblesoft's *New Exhaustive Strong's Numbers and Concordance with Expanded Greek-Hebrew Dictionary*, s.v. "*entugchano*," NT:1793.

11. Desmond T. Evans, *Devotional* Living (N.p: N.d).

12. Ibid., s.v. "*deesis*," NT:1162, and "*deomai*," NT:1189.

13. Ibid., s.v. "*energeo*," NT:1754.

14. Jack Hayford, ed., *New Spirit-Filled Life Bible* (Nashville: Thomas Nelson, 2002), s.v. "Matthew 11:12," 1309.

15. Ibid., "Kingdom Dynamics: Matthew 16:16," 1420.

16. Ibid., s.v. "Psalm 1:2," 686.

17. Biblesoft's *New Exhaustive Strong's Numbers and Concordance with Expanded Greek-Hebrew Dictionary*, s.v. "*hagah*," OT:1897.

18. Helen Mendes Love, *Reflections on the Upsides of Aging* (Nashville: WestBow Press, 2011), 77–78.

Chapter 6—The Anointing to Prophesy

1. Hayford, ed., *New Spirit-Filled Life Bible*, 1842.

2. As described by Morgan, *100 Bible Verses Everyone Should Know by Heart*, 4. Viewed at Google Books.

3. James Allen, *As a Man Thinketh* (Rockville, MD: Arc Manor, 2007), 24–25. Viewed at Google Books.

4. Labri.org, "Learning From Francis Schaeffer," http://www.labri .org/england/resources/Learning-from-Francis-Schaeffer.pdf (accessed April 9, 2013).

Chapter 7—The Warfare Anointing

1. Mike Murdock, *7 Decisions That Decide Your Success in Life* (Fort Worth, TX: The Wisdom Center, 2010). Viewed at Google Books.

2. BBC.com, "2003: 'War Criminal' Idi Amin Dies," On This Day: 16 August, http://news.bbc.co.uk/onthisday/hi/dates/stories/august/16/ newsid_3921000/3921361.stm (accessed April 9, 2013).

3. *New Vision*, "Live Updates: Uganda Celebrates Golden Jubilee," www. newvision.co.ug, October 9, 2012, http://www.newvision .co.ug/news/636203-live-updats-uganda-celebrates-golden -jubilee.html (accessed April 9, 2013). Used by permission.

4. Written by Bob Gesing specifically for this book.

5. While I do not remember the name of the author and title of blog, the quotes are from Charles Levinson and Adam Entous, "Israel's

Iron Dome Defense Battled to Get Off Ground," *Wall Street Journal*, November 26, 2012, http://online.wsj.com/article/SB1000142412788732 471250457813693107846821O.html (accessed April 9, 2013).

6. J. Wilbur Chapman, as quoted in David Jeremiah, *Slaying the Giants in Your Life* (Nashville: Thomas Nelson, 2001), 92. Viewed at Google Books.

CHAPTER 8—THE UNCTION TO FUNCTION

1. Written by Shirley Arnold specifically for this book.
2. David Platt, *Radical Together* (Colorado Springs, CO: Multnomah, 2011), 80.
3. *Webster's American Family Dictionary*, s.v. "sanctify."
4. *Strong's Talking Greek and Hebrew Dictionary*, s.v. "*mishḥâ*," OT:4888.
5. Ibid., s.v. "*chrisma*," NT:5545.
6. *Vine's Expository Dictionary of Old and New Testament Words*, s.v. "*chrisma*."
7. *Webster's American Family Dictionary*, s.v. "unction."
8. Written by Karen Wheaton specifically for this book.
9. Written by Rod Parsley specifically for this book.
10. *Strong's Talking Greek and Hebrew Dictionary*, s.v. "*praotēs*," NT:4236.

CHAPTER 9—THE ANOINTING TO CHANGE SOCIETY AND CULTURE

1. ThinkExist.com, "H. Jackson Brown, Jr. Quotes," http://thinkexist. com/quotes/H._Jackson_Brown,_Jr./ (accessed April 10, 2013).
2. Alex Murashko, "10th Anniversary Edition of 'The Purpose Driven Life' Redesigned for Millennials," *Christian Post*, June 14, 2012, http:// www.christianpost.com/news/10th-anniversary -edition-of-the-purpose-driven-life-redesigned-for-millennials -76623/ (accessed April 10, 2013).
3. *Strong's Talking Greek and Hebrew Dictionary*, s.v. "*spoudē*," NT:4710.
4. John Charles Ryle, *Consider Your Ways: Being a Pastor's Address to His Flock* (London: Hunt and Son, 1849), 4–5, emphasis added. Viewed at Google Books.
5. The Salvation Army, "History of The Salvation Army," http://salva-tionarmycareers.com/jobboard/SalvationArmyCareers/without_fl/his-tory.htm (accessed April 10, 2013). Permission to quote requested.

6. The Salvation Army, "Programs That Help," http://www
.salvationarmyusa.org/usn/www_usn_2.nsf/vw-local/programs
(accessed April 10, 2013).

7. The Salvation Army, "History," http://web.salvationarmy.org/ihq/
www_sa.nsf/vw-sublinks/5622f771bd70a75a80256d4e003ae0a3
(accessed April 10, 2013); The Salvation Army, "Salvation Army
Installs Israel L. Gaither as National Commander and Eva D. Gaither
as National President of Women's Ministries in USA," http://web.sal-
vationarmy.org/ihq/www_sa.nsf/vw-news/
0e323c311e9cc3738025716c004e9a37 (accessed April 10, 2013).

8. Author unknown, "Carrots, Eggs, or Coffee: Which One Are You?"
This story can be found on many blogs and sites on the Internet.

9. As quoted in Raymond F. Culpepper, *The Great Commission Con-
nection* (Cleveland, TN: Pathway Press, 2011), 138. Viewed at Google
Books.

10. Author unknown, "John 3:16." This story can be found in numerous
sites on the Internet.

CHAPTER 10—THE MENTORING ANOINTING

1. *Strong's Talking Greek and Hebrew Dictionary*, s.v. "Iēsous," NT:2424.

2. Ibid., s.v. "Christos," NT:5547.

3. Written by Bishop Harry R. Jackson Jr. specifically for this book.

4. Hayford, ed., "Kingdom Dynamics: 2:12–14, Growth in Stages," *New
Spirit-Filled Life Bible*, 1785.

5. Jackie Kendall, *The Mentoring Mom: 11 Ways to Model Christ for
Your Child* (N.p.: New Hope Publishers, 2006), 161. Viewed at Google
Books.

6. Ibid.

CHAPTER 11—THE ANOINTING TO PROSPER

1. Winston Churchill, "Humanity Will Not Be Cast Down," speech
given October 10, 1908, in Dundee, Scotland, as recorded in Martin
Gilbert, ed., *Churchill: The Power of Words* (Boston: Da Capo Press,
2012), 63. Viewed at Google Books.

2. Deena Marie Carr, *The Carr Guide to Personal Wealth* (Charlotte,
NC: Lifebridge Books, 2012).

3. Ibid., my paraphrase.

4. Ibid.

5. *Strong's Talking Greek and Hebrew Dictionary*, s.v. "*miqreh*," OT:4745.

6. *Webster's American Family Dictionary*, s.v. "happen."

7. Perry Stone shared this with me in a conversation.

8. *Strong's Talking Greek and Hebrew Dictionary*, s.v. "*merimnaō*," NT:3309.

9. Hayford, ed., "Word Wealth: 6:25," *New Spirit-Filled Life Bible*, 1301.

10. Ibid., "Word Wealth: 145:2," 797.

11. *Webster's American Family Dictionary*, s.v. "iniquity."

12. Hayford, ed., "Word Wealth: 52:9," *New Spirit-Filled Life Bible*, 935.

Chapter 12—Misconceptions and Misuses of the Anointing

1. Alexander Kelly McClure, *"Abe" Lincoln's Yarns and Stories* (New York: Western W. Wilson, 1901), 184. Viewed at Google Books.

2. Iverna Tompkins, *The Holy and the Profane* (N.p.: Gospel Outreach Publishers, 1975), "The Issue," chapter 1; viewed at Iverna Tompkins Ministries, Part 1, http://www.ivernainternational .com/teaching/hap01.php (accessed April 12, 2013).

3. Ibid., "The Profane," chapter 2.

4. Ibid.

5. Ibid., viewed at Iverna Tompkins Ministries, Part 2, http:// ivernainternational.com/teaching/hap02.php (accessed April 12, 2013).

6. Written by Martha Munizzi specifically for this book.

7. Smithsonian Institution, "The Hope Diamond," http://www .si.edu/Encyclopedia_SI/nmnh/hope.htm (accessed April 12, 2013).

8. Desmond Evans, *The Beauty of Holiness Notes* (N.p.: N.d.).

9. *Strong's Talking Greek and Hebrew Dictionary*, s.v. "*zûr*," OT:2114.

10. Ibid., s.v. "*'ēsh*," OT:784.

11. *Barnes' Notes*, electronic database, copyright © 1997 by Biblesoft, s.v. "Leviticus 10:2."

12. Chambers, *My Utmost for His Highest*, "February 8."

13. Written by Wes Tuttle specifically for this book.

14. Written by Cheryl Gesing specifically for this book.

Conclusion—Staying in the Flow of the Anointing

1. Jonathan Cahn, *The Harbinger* (Lake Mary, FL: FrontLine, 2011), 250.

2. Written by Desmond Evans specifically for this book.

"I want you to be the exception to the norm. I want you to become a powerful example to others. I want you to be mighty in your spirit, whole through and through, and able to stand up in adversity."

—JUDY JACOBS

978-0-88419-958-8 | US $13.99

978-1-59979-233-0 | US $14.99

978-1-59979-066-4 | US $14.99

Faith that stands firm in the face of opposition

Become confident in your calling and prevail against all odds

It's never too late to live your best